Reflections on Dalit and Minorities Issues: An Anthology

Reflections on Dalit and Minorities Issues: An Anthology

Edited by:

Prof. Mohd. Mujtaba Khan

Dr. K.R. Narayanan Centre for Dalit and Minorities Studies, Jamia Millia Islamia, New Delhi

in association with

KANISHKA PUBLISHERS, DISTRIBUTORS
NEW DELHI-110 002

KANISHKA PUBLISHERS, DISTRIBUTORS
4697/5-21 A, Ansari Road, Daryaganj
New Delhi-110 002
Phones : 2327 0497, 2328 8285
Fax : 011-2328 8285
e-mail: kanishka_publishing@yahoo.co.in

First Published 2007

ISBN 978-81-7391-999-2

PRINTED IN INDIA

Published by Madan Sachdeva for Kanishka Publishers, Distributors, 4697/5-21A, Ansari Road, Daryaganj, New Delhi-110 002, Typeset by Sunshine Graphics, Delhi, and Printed at Nice Printing Press, Delhi.

JAMIA MILLIA ISLAMIA

(A Central University by an Act of Parliament)

Professor Mushirul Hasan

Ph.D. (Cantab)

Vice-Chancellor

Maulana Mohammed Ali Jauhar Marg New Delhi-110025

Email: mushirulhasan@yahoo.com-vc@jmi.ernet.in

Tel. 26984650, 26985180 Fax. 00-91-11-26981232 Gram: JAMIA website: http://www.jmi.nic.in

Foreword

I am happy to introduce the first publication of the Dr. K.R. Narayanan Centre for Dalit and Minorities Studies titled, 'Reflections on Dalit and Minorities Issues: An Anthology'.

This volume is an outcome of the Occasional Papers commissioned by the Centre on various thematic issues related to dalits and minorities in India. The literature emanating from diverse sources is extremely rich, insightful and reflective of the contemporary researches.

The debates presented in the volume are an important contribution of the Centre, not only towards knowledge generation, but simultaneously, towards the visibility that Dalit and Minority related issues have generated, both in the academia and the civil society in contemporary times.

The tapestry of this volume has been weaved from a broad spectrum of contributors. They include prominent academicians, besides other writers.

I feel this volume would be immensely useful not only to the academia, civil society, government and researchers, but also the laymen who are concerned with issues related to poverty, social exclusion and marginality.

Prof. Mohammed Mujtaba Khan, the Director of Dr. K.R. Narayanan Centre for Dalit and Minorities Studies along with all team deserve congratulations for making this publication possible. I hope that the Centre will continue to uphold the traditions of academic vigour.

Mushirul Hasan.

(Mushirul Hasan)

Introduction

Dalit and Minorities representing caste and religious identities have come to occupy a central place in the socio-political discourse and academic discussions in modern India. Curiously enough even political parties both, major and minor have started taking interest in Dalit and Minorities issues as a part of their electoral strategies to make political fortunes at the hustings. Caste and religious identities have become so pronounced that other variables such as economy and development have assumed a secondary or supplementary role. While caste divides the populace horizontally, religion provides a basis for vertical splits between communities in terms of their interests entailing vested interests to exploit the situtation and polarize the society on communal lines.

In the realm of India's social history, the caste oppressed and community oppressed manifested commonalities in their quest and struggle both for employment and educational opportunities. They perceived the entrenched castes as their adversaries who have been orchestrating a reign of oppression and subjugation treating repression as a part of their heritage. Any defiance of the traditional hierarchical norm amounts to ghettorization. The caste-oppressed and the community-oppressed came to be fed on myths about each other, implanted and perpetrated by the vested interests. Often the one has been deployed against the other leading to distortions and fragmentations in the social scenario that has acquired alarming proportions in the recent years.

It was believed that the socio-political values of Renaissance that developed in the course of the Independence Movement would usher in a secular democratic society in India. Unfortunately this did not happen. On the contrary, divisive tendencies came to cannibalize on the very notions of secularism and democracy. Independent India, particularly post-Nehruvian phase witnessed pronounced casteist hatred and antagonistic communal consciousness often manifesting into sectarian and communal frenzy. The constantly escalating tyranny of the traditionally dominant castes and communal groups on the one hand and the growing enlightenment among the Dalits and the Minorities about their legitimate rights, particularly among their new generation youth, frequently leading to rise of violence such as Khairlanji and other incidents, warrants a paradigmatic shift to address these issues and in this context, Dr. K. R. Narayanan Centre for Dalit and Minorities Studies, Jamia Millia Islamia, conceived and established by Vice-Chancellor, Padma Shri Prof. Mushirul Hasan is a modest step.

Recognizing the caste-oppressed and the community excluded as an extension and elaboration of the new concepts of Human Rights, Social Development and Distributive Democracy and Justice, the Centre operating as a think tank has been generating academic debates and discussions, formulating them in a non-partisan and plural manner within a framework of egalitarian social solidarity as its ideal in terms of the 'Rights Approach' and inter-disciplinary focus to the problems of Dalits, Minorities and other excluded strata of society.

This anthology of essays, *Reflections on Dalit and Minorities Issues* is one such effort in the direction of accomplishing the centre's objectives. The volume addresses several key themes concerning Dalit and Minorities issues. Some of these papers have a comparative focus. The themes are diverse covering a wide range of issues such as; the idea of Dalit Muslims, minority rights in South Asia, Dalit Movement in Andhra Pradesh, the idea of sacred prostitute, the contribution of Dr. Ambedkar on education movement in India and many others.

Prof. Imtiaz Ahmad, renowned political sociologist, seeks to explain one of the most intriguing puzzles concerning social stratification among Indian Muslims specifically the segment called Dalit Muslims. Ahmad while making a persuasive case of widespread ambiguity that determines the nature of discourse revolving around the notion of Dalit Muslims also effers an adquate amount of discussion on how Mandal Commission has contributed to the ambiguity pertaining to the idea of Dalit Muslims. While expressing his uneasiness with the current research, Ahmad calls for a "rich and ethnographic research" on the caste question of Indian Muslims, and suggests that such research must pay attention to the attitudes of non-*arzal* towards *arzal* and makes an assessment of internal discrimination towards *arzals*.

James Massey in his contribution, *Minority Rights in the South Asian Countries with Special Reference to India* documents comparative insights to the issue of minority rights in different countries like Pakistan, Bangladesh, Nepal, Sri Lanka at the same time evaluating constitutional provisions in these societies to make an assessment of Minority rights. He further argues, "that the Indian Constitution with regard to the religious minorities offers a best model in the world" at the same time recognizes various violations in different states of India like Gujarat, Madhya Pradesh, West Bengal, Orissa, Punjab and other places in which Minorities particularly Muslims and Christians have paid great prices with their lives and properties.

Prof. A Satyanarayana's, *Articulation of Self and the Other: Emergence of the Dalit Movement in Andhra Pradesh,* provides insights on Dalit Movement by focusing on the life and contributions of a select Dalit intellectuals and activists. According to the author, the formation of Adi-Andhra Mahasabha in 1917 marked the collective self-mobilization of Dalits for self-respect, dignity, equality and justice. The author at length argues that despite a powerful and long tradition of Dalit Movement, Dalits in Andhra Pradesh continue to remain an object of hatred among caste Hindus.

Prof. Raj Sekhar Basu in his *Complexities of the Dalit Movement in India* documents various interpretations of caste identity and their impact on the Dalit Movement in India. He argues that the usage of the terms such as "national community" and "national culture" reflect the story of upper caste dominations over different sub-altern social groups within the nation.

Prof. K.S. Chalam in his *Dr. B.R. Ambedkar and the People's Education Movement in India* presents an idepth analysis of the contributions of iconic Dalit leader, Dr. B.R. Ambedkar specifically in relation to mass education and offers a succinct account of Dr. Ambedkar's evolution as a scholar and philosopher under the influence of Professor John Dewey and Mahatma Phooley.

Prof. R. K. Kale's essay *Special Schemes of UGC for Empowerment of SCs/STs* while providing a narrative of the institutions and schemes for the empowerment of the SCs and STs explains how the UGC seeks to address the issue of social deprivation by setting special cells in the universities to ensure effective implementation of reservation policy. He also analyses how remedial coaching centres help overcome students' inadequacies owing to their caste background and equip them to compete with others not only in Civil Serives but also for the NET examination and entry into the public services. Citing studies that examined the impact of the UGC schemes, he believes that the UGC schemes are a great source of benefit to the SCs and STs despite continuing practice of discrimination.

Priyadarhsini Vijaisri's, *Purity and Pollution: Situating the Outcaste Sacred Prostitute in a Hindu Regional Tradition* offers a historical narrative of the tradition of sacred prostitution. She argues that the custom of sacred prostition encompasses women from various cultural groups representing an interface of caste-outscaste religious traditions that draws in its fold the dominant Sudra, the lower Sudra the lower Sudra and the Outcastes. The pervasiveness of the tradition is its power to draw Divinities worshipped by distinct caste and outcaste groups.

I thank all the contributors to this volume and express indebtness to my colleagues, Mr. Mujibur Rehman, Visiting Professor and Mr. Prashant Negi, the most dynamic young lecturer in this Centre, for their cooperation in compiling this anthology.

Prof. Mohd. Mujtaba Khan

Contents

List of Contributors

Imtiaz Ahmad has been Professor of Political Sociology at the Centre for Political Studies, Jawaharlal Nehru University, New Delhi. Prof. Ahmad edited many path breaking works. *Caste and Social Stratification Among Muslims* (1973); *Divorce and Remarriage Among Muslims in India* (2003) and *Pluralism and Equality: Values in Indian Society and Politics,* with Partha S. Ghosh and Helmut Reifeld (2000).

James Massey is the Director of the Centre for Dalit/Subaltern Studies, New Delhi. He was Member of the National Commission for Minorities, Government of India. Prof. Massey authored many works. *Minorities in a Democracy – The Indian Experience* (1999); *Rights of Minorities to Religious Freedom* (1999); *Rights of the Minorities to Establish and Administer Educational Institutions* (1998).

A. Satyanarayana is Professor of History, Osmania University, Hyderabad. Prof. Satyanarayana is currently Visiting Professor at University of Kyoto, Japan. His works include, *Andhra Peasants under Bristish Rule* (1992) and *Dalit and Upper Castes: Essays on Social History* (2005).

Raj Sekhar Basu taught History at Rabindra Bharathi University, and currently associated with the Department of History, University of Calcutta. His Ph.D. was on "Socio-Cultural Transformation of the Christian Communities – Pulayar and Paraiyars in South India."

K.S. Chalam has been Professor of Economics at Andhra University, Waltair. He was Vice-Chancellor, Dravidian University, Kuppam, and currently Member, UPSC. His works include: *Education and Weaker Sections* (1988); *Relevance of Ambedkarism in India* (1993) *and Globalisation and the Future of Dalits* (2003).

R.K. Kale is Professor of Life Sciences, Jawaharlal Nehru University, New Delhi. Prof. Kale contributes regularly in reputed journals on educational aspects of the marginalized groups. He is currently Dean of Students at JNU.

Priyadarshini Vijaisri, currently Visiting Associate Fellow, Centre for the Study of Developing Societies, Delhi; she had been Fellow at International Institute for Asian Studies, Leiden. Her works include: *Recasting the Devadasi: Patterns of Sacred Prostitution in Colonial South India* (2004).

1

Can There be a Category Called Dalit Muslims?

IMTIAZ AHMAD

On the face of it, the expression 'Dalit Muslims' would appear to be a contradiction in terms. It is commonly held that Islam is an egalitarian religion and there are no status differences among Muslims. As such, there is no question of the prevalence of untouchability among them and a category called 'Dalit Muslims' cannot be said to exist. This is the standard line that is handed down whenever any reference to 'Dalit Muslims' is made.

This would be a perfectly understandable position to take were it not for the fact that considerable evidence exists to suggest that a category called "Dalit Muslims' does exist in India. Ghaus Ansari argued on the basis of evidence from the decennial censuses that Muslims in India were divided into three broad categories that he called the *ashraf* (noble born), *ajlaf* (mean and lowly) and *arzal* (excluded).[1] Each of these categories was further divided into a number of groups which, following the practice of the decennial censuses, he chose to designate as castes. Since Ansari was relying on the evidence supplied by the decennial censuses, he could not examine the process of mutual interaction among these castes. He generally suggested that the three broad categories he had identified constituted a hierarchy in which the castes were ranked in an order of social precedence. How this hierarchy was constituted and what was the basis on which the rank order was settled were questions that Ansari could not discuss on account of the limitations of the data he used.

More focused research on social stratification among Muslims in the early seventies and subsequently relied upon empirical methods, painstakingly collecting information on actual, day-to-day interactions among the Muslim communities.[2] This research succeeded in providing a more grounded picture of the situation of the groups whom Ansari had called *arzal*. It demonstrated that in terms of day-to-day social interactions the *arzal* existed on the margins of society. Even so, the range of dimensions of interaction that this research explored was restricted to areas of commensality, endogamy and sociality. It showed that the *arzal* engaged in the lowly occupation of scavenging, confined their marriages within the group and were excluded in the villages as well as the towns into separate residential quarters in which members of the other categories did not live. This research also noted the existence among the *arzal* communities of a system of internal government and social control with a hereditary official who regulated the life of group members and punished any transgressions of group norms besides settling domestic or intra-group disputes. Since much of this early research was focused on local communities, villages and towns, and covered groups falling into what Ansari had designated as *arzal* and *ajlaf*, the range of information on the *arzal* communities does not go beyond this limited range. For example, it is silent on the exclusion of the *arzal* communities in the ritual and religious spheres as well as on whether the religious specialists who cater to the *ashraf* and *ajlaf* communities also minister to them.

One question raised by this research was how the presence of groups whom Ansari had called *arzal* be explained. Should they be seen in strictly occupational terms as practitioners of a distinct occupation that in their case happened to be lowly and demeaning without status connotations? Or, should it be seen as arising from more fundamental and intrinsic considerations requiring evaluation of groups into a ranked social order? Opinions on this significant point were substantially determined by how one viewed the position of Islam in relation to social stratification. Those who took the position that Islam was against any social stratification and posited the inherent equality of all human beings tended to represent the presence of *arzal* communities as merely an occupational division without any status implications.[3] From their point of view, the disabilities and exclusion characterizing the *arzal* communities applied to individuals and were relevant only in the occupational realm. Once their members move outside the occupational realm they are on par with everyone else. Others did not flatly take the position that Islam was against social stratification. They viewed the existence of *arzal* communities as reflecting a system in which groups were ranked as superior and inferior and individuals carried the burden of their group status through having to suffer disabilities and exclusion as members of groups.

Since the most elaborate expression of a system of social stratification wherein groups are ranked as superior or inferior and individuals are forced to carry the burden of their group status is found in the caste system, one way of characterizing the presence of *arzal* communities could be in terms of caste. However, since Islam in popular imagination is seen as the harbinger of social inequality, such characterization is open to contestation on ideological grounds. This has precisely been happening in sociological research on the *arzal* communities. At the behavioural level, sociologists are willing to concede that there are elements of caste in Indo-Muslim society. However, as soon as the discussion shifts from behaviour to ideology they recoil from their position, seeking to add caveats or hedge around the issue by admitting unabashedly that when they apply the term in the context of a Muslim group they are using it in a loose sense. Two recent writings by Husnain[4] and Nazir exemplify this tendency most eloquently.

Husnain locates his discussion in the context of the question whether the concept of caste can be applied to the system of social stratification of a community professing a faith other than Hinduism. His conclusion is bald and simple: 'It is true that the egalitarian social order of Islam stands in sharp contrast with the ideology of caste yet the 'Indian Islam' and 'Hindu Caste System' have been able to achieve a substantial compatibility'.[5] He then goes on to offer a host of explanations for why this should be the case. He writes:[6]

Hutton sounds convincing when he says that when Muslims and Christians came to India, the caste was in the air and the followers of even these egalitarian ideologies could note escape the infection of caste. Moreover, the overwhelming majority of Indian Muslim population comes form the lower Hindu castes who have been coming into the fold of Islam to escape from social persecution and the oppressive socio-economic disabilities. They were also attracted and lured by the social egalitarianism of Islam but the search for equality proved a mirage. In many cases there were improvements in their socio-economic condition yet the goal of social equality remained illusive. Moreover, in most of the cases the people embracing Islam gave up their religious faith but not the caste that was brought forward even to a new socio-religious milieu. Thus, it would be apt to say that while Islam may not be having castes or caste-like groupings, the Indian Muslims do have.

No sooner that he has made this sociological formulation, Husnain becomes uncomfortable. As if fearing that he might have committed an almost sacrilegious act by declaring that there is caste among Indian Muslims, he wishes to recoil from it. Cryptically, he adds:[7]

> But in the present paper an attempt is being made to stay clear of the issue whether the model of social stratification among the Indian Muslims is the replica of the Hindu caste system or not. The author, in this paper, shall be using the term caste and caste system among the Indian Muslims in a conveniently loose manner. It is undisputed that there are groups of people among the Muslims who are organised more or less like the Hindu castes but this is also true that many of them are less rigid because Islam, theoretically at least, permits marriage between different classes of believers.

Not only that. He looks for crutches that would enable him to perform this summersault. He finds one in the following statement of Nazir, which he quotes approvingly:

> ...It is necessary to make a distinction between a caste system and caste labels: the former refers to a local system of hierarchically ordered corporate groupings involving division of labour, occupational specialisation, unequal dependence, and recruitment by birth only; the latter refers to a set of non-local, non-corporate named groups which provide a ranking hierarchy, and which do not involve occupational specialisation, unequal dependence, and recruitment by birth only.[8]

'Perhaps,' concludes Husnain, 'the "caste system' and "caste like groupings" among the Indian Muslims with all its fluidity may be better analysed and better understood through this observation'.

This assumes that Hindus live under 'the caste system'. Muslims only use castes labels. Several theoretical and empirical questions are raised by this assumption. First, how is this assumption made? Is it made on the basis of a piece of empirical research? Or, is it made on entirely a priori grounds. As far as I am aware, there has to date been no empirical research which can be said to have established beyond the shadow of a doubt that Muslims do not live under a caste system and only use caste labels. Indeed, if such empirical research existed, the dilemma these authors (and others) face over how to characterise Muslim social stratification in India would not exist. It exists because available empirical research has demonstrated that social stratification of Muslim communities in India and beyond is marked by features of the caste system. It is, therefore, clear that the assumption is made on a priori grounds. As believing Muslims committed to upholding the widely proclaimed Islamic egalitarianism as axiomatic, they cannot face up to the behavioural reality that Muslims live under a caste system. They not only assume the distinction between 'the caste system' and 'caste labels' but go on to suggest that it constitutes a viable framework for analysing and understanding Muslim social stratification in India. It is used as a smokescreen to avoid facing the harsh behavioural reality of caste among Muslims in India.

Second, is there an empirical basis to the assertion that Muslim social organisation in India is 'a set of non-local, nor-corporate named groups which provide a ranking hierarchy, and which do not involve occupational specialisation, unequal dependence, and recruitment by birth only'?[9] Nazir does not make explicit the level at which he is talking. Is he talking about the categorisation of Muslims into the broad categories of ashraf, ajlaf and arzal? If that is his point of reference, then his characterisation of Muslim social organisation as a set of non-local, non-corporate groups can be said to have some validity. However, it would invalidate the distinction between 'the caste system' and 'caste labels' since similar broad division exists in the form of varna categories in 'the caste system'. Ansari used the three broad categories of ashraf, ajlaf and arzal in the collective sense but clearly recognised that they were divided into smaller named groups that were distinguished from one another by occupation, endogamy and sociability. Thus, if Nazir's reference is to the groups at this level, then his description of Muslim groups is wholly erroneous. Let us look closely at the empirical evidence in order to determine whether the distinction he posits between 'the caste system' and 'caste labels', and by implication between Hindu and Muslim modes of social organisation, is confirmed by available studies.

Sociological research on Muslims in India as opposed to lay and impressionistic writings continues to be thin. Evidence brought together by Ahmad (1973) and subsequent research demonstrates that Muslim groups, which are the point of reference here, for which words biradari and zat are commonly used, are local and corporate entities. Even biradaris or zata such as Saiyyid, Sheikh and Ansaris, which are dispersed widely and found in different parts of a district, state or the county, are identified by their affiliation to a particular territory and restrict their marriages to members within that territory. Of course, how that territory is distinguished varies widely. For Sayyids, Shiekhs and Pathans, which resent being characterised as biradaris and prefer to be described as zats, the association to territory are expressed through appending the name of the territory to its name. Thus, one hears of Sayyids of Satrikh, Sheikhs of Allahabad, Kidwais of Baragaon or Kasauli and Pathans of Malihabad. In the case of biradaris that have an internal organisation of government and social control (called biradari or zat panchayat) this territorial association is defined by the jurisdiction of the biradari panchayat. The Ansaris in Rasulpur, where I carried out fieldwork, were divided into concentric circles of three and thirteen villages. They confined their marriages to thirteen villages though Ansaris existed in neighbouring areas as well.

This is not all. Considerable evidence exists to show that the biradaris or zats are associated with particular occupations, are inter-dependent (tied into patron-client relationships of the jajmani type), and are endogamous. This does not mean that all members of a biradari or zat necessarily practice the occupation with which their group is traditionally associated. There has been much variation throughout history among biradaris and zats, as indeed there has been within castes, in the extent to which their members remain tied to the practice of their traditional occupation. Biradaris and zats higher up in the social hierarchy did not usually have a traditional occupation and there was no close association between biradari or zat and traditional occupation. On the other hand, biradaris and zats further down the social ladder had traditional occupations and their association with occupation was strong. This was not significantly different from the picture of groups in what Nazir would characterise as 'the caste system'. Risley's following observation makes this explicit: [10]

> In theory each caste has a distinctive occupation, but it does not follow that its members practise this traditional occupation... The traditional occupation of the Brahmans is the priesthood, but in practice they follow all manner of pursuits. Many are clerks or cooks, while some are soldiers, lawyers, shop-keeprs and even day-labourers, but they remain Brahmans all the same. The Chamars of Bihar are workers in skin, but in Orissa they are toddy-drawers. In Orissa and the south of Gaya the Dhobi is often a hewer of splitter of wood. In Bihar and Bengal the Dom is a scavenger or basket maker, but in the Orissa states he is a drummer or basket maker and has nothing to do with the removal of night soil: in Chittagong and Assam he is a fisherman, in Cashmere a cultivator and in Kumaon a stone mason.

The argument that Muslim groups, biradaris and zats, are not based on recruitment by birth only is equally fallacious. Like the groups in what Nazir would call 'the caste system', Muslim biradaris and zats are based on recruitment by birth only. There is no process by which one can become a Saiyid, Sheikh or Julaha except that of birth. It is for this reason that when someone marries into another biradari or zat, he is not integrated into another biradari or zat but retains his or her original biradari or zat association. There exists a possibility in the case of biradaris and zats to attempt social mobility and end up becoming a Sayid, Sheikh or Pathan in course of time through inventing a rationale and a genealogy. Where such social mobility occurs, the basis of recruitment to the biradari or zat does not change. The biradari or zat just ends up becoming another biradari or zat, and comes to be known by another name, to which recruitment continues to be based on the principle of birth. This is again not significantly different from the situation in 'the caste system' where castes have the possibility of changing their antecedents and name through the process of social mobility. Thus, the point that both the biradaris and zats are 'less rigid because Islam, theoretically at least, permits marriage between different classes of believers'[11] is not empirically established. It is commonly asserted without a substantial basis in any empirical research.

This raises fundamental questions. Why Husnain and Nazir as well as a host of other researchers who have worked on the sensitive question of the existence of caste among Muslims are so strongly persuaded to posit that there are significant differences between 'the caste system' and the system of biradaris and zats? Is it that these differences actually exist but empirical research has so far failed to unearth them? Or, is it that they are persuaded into asserting these differences contrary to empirical evidence out of extraneous considerations? Is it that they are prone to emphasising these differences because as believing Muslims they are familiar with the Islamic discourse that asserts that Islam preaches social equality and are afraid to take a contrary position? Or, is it that asserting these differences is a defence mechanism whereby they can simultaneously adhere to their disciplinary obligation as social scientists as well as their religious obligation to uphold what is commonly considered the Islamic view on social stratification? My own view has been that the tendency to emphasise differences between 'the caste system' and the system of biradaris and zats arises from some such considerations, but I would refrain from making any such point here. I would like, instead to explore whether their starting point that Islam is an egalitarian religion and preaches social equality theologically and sociologically valid. This is central to understanding their standpoint.

There is need to ask three different questions of the Islamic text if we are to understand Islam's position with respect to social stratification and social equality. First, whether Islam is opposed to social stratification as such or is merely opposed to social inequality. Second, what is truly the Islamic attitude towards social inequality that existed in the society in which Islam evolved and took root. Finally, whether the social equality that it proclaims, and to which reference is always made when it is suggested that Islam is an egalitarian religion, is a description of an existing state of affairs in society or is merely an ideal that is given to mankind as a direction in which it should strive. It is necessary to ask these questions in order to understand the nature of the emphasis on egalitarianism and social equality in Islam. Basic to these questions is the sociological dictum that no society beyond the most primitive in the sense of lacking any kind of economic surplus can be truly egalitarian. This was the point at the heart of Veblen's Theory of the Leisured Class wherein he argued that as societies generated economic surplus there almost always developed some form of social stratification. Of course, Veblen's concern was an analysis of the lifestyle and consumption pattern of the class that controlled the economic surplus and the symbolic and behavioural expressions of its privileged position. Even so, the substantive theoretical point of his analysis was that once a society starts generating economic surplus some form of social stratification is bound to emerge. Pitirim A. Sorokin articulated this point as a general statement:[12]

Any organised social group is always a stratified social body. There has not been and does not exist any permanent social group which is "flat", and in which all members are equal. Unstratified society, with a real equality of its members, is a myth, which has never been realised in the history of mankind. This statement may sound paradoxical and yet it is accurate. The forms and proportions of stratification vary, but its essence is permanent, as far as any permanent and organised social group is concerned."

On even the most casual reading of the Islamic scriptural text one is struck that quite irrespective of the emphasis it places on equality of human beings Islam's orientation is remarkably hierarchical. Its hierarchical orientation comes in a wide variety of fields. First, the relationship of the believers with non-believers is conceived in strictly hierarchical terms with the believer, the dhimmi and the kafir constituting a clear hierarchy. Second, the relationship of Allah to the believer is conceived in hierarchical terms. It is a relationship of subordination and subservience so much so that the individual believer must prostrate before Allah in daily prayers and must at the same time see himself as utterly powerless in relation to Him. Any number of passages exist in the Islamic scriptural text that endorse the relatively lowly standing of the believers, whether as individuals or as a collective entity, in relation to Allah. Second, the relationship of the wife to her husband is clearly conceived in hierarchical terms even if the text does not distinguish between them in terms of the religious duties enjoined upon them. This is sometimes cited by Muslim feminists and Muslim modernists to argue that Islam guarantees equality of gender and does not place a Muslim woman in any inferior position to a man. However, in reality a woman is subordinate to a man and the relationship between them is seen as constituting a hierarchy wherein the woman stands in relation to a man in the same position as the individual stands in relation to the community and the community stands in relation to Allah. Fatima Mernissi characterises this orientation of Islam in relation to women by the concept of nusuz, which implies an unequal relationship. Islam makes a distinction between the wives of the Prophet and other women and the responsibilities placed on them are also distinctly varied. Indeed, the Quranic verse that orthodoxy used at a later stage in the development of Islam to impose the custom of veiling for Muslim women originally related to the wives of the Prophet. Finally, the relationship between the master and slave is conceived in clearly hierarchical terms even if the master is called upon to deal with the slave with kindness and merit is assigned to those who would free their slaves. Thus, it is clear that the framework of Islamic thinking is deeply imbued with the notion of hierarchy and social stratification.

It is true that the Arab society in which Islam evolved did not possess great differences of wealth, but economic differentiation between ordinary Bedouins and the trading classes did exist. One can easily imagine that they would have differed with respect to their wealth, material possessions and lifestyles and Islam could not have brushed them under the carpet. It would have been required to deal with them, as they would have been reflected in their behaviour and mutual attitudes. As far as the Islamic scriptural text is concerned, it clearly recognises such distinctions in society and prescribes appropriate forms of behaviour for each. It asks those deprived in social and economic terms to be content and to live according to their means. It is repeatedly said in the text that Allah is All-seeing and would reward the poor for their poverty on the day of judgement. At the same time, the wealthy and rich, while they are allowed to live in their riches and to spend according to their economic standing, are warned not to be too proud of their material possessions. Moreover, they are asked to show kindness to those who are deprived and poor and to part with a portion of their wealth and income for the poor. Even the poor are conceived in hierarchical terms: first come the near ones followed by orphans and then the destitute and the deprived. If some kind of social stratification had not existed in society, Islamic scriptural text would neither have referred to those differences, nor indicated appropriate forms of behaviour for them. It would also not have sought to device an economic framework for the redistribution of wealth in a manner that the poor and able to meet both ends meet. It is, thus, clear that the emphasis that Islamic scriptural text places on social equality does not describe an existing state of affairs.

If the worldview of the Islamic scriptural text is hierarchical and it admits of social and economic differences in society, then how should we interpret its emphasis upon social equality? One way to interpret this can be to ignore that Islamic orientation is hierarchical and to argue that it stands for egalitarianism as an absolute value. I would argue that those who maintain that Islam contemplates no social stratification are interpreting Islam in precisely this way. Even when they encounter social differentiation and stratification, they glibly ignore it and flash the proclaimed egalitarianism of Islam as a social reality. The other way of interpretation can be to recognise a fundamental difference. This is the difference between the societies as it exists and as it ought to exist and to maintain that the Islamic proclamation in favour of social equality is more in the nature of an ideal for the future than a description of an existing state of affairs. My own position is that drawing this distinction is important in any consideration of the question of the presence or absence of caste and caste-based social stratification in Indo-Muslim society. It enables us to see that a distinction has to be made between the society which exists, and where caste- or class-based distinctions may exist, and a future state of society where they are expected to disappear and give rise to an egalitarian society. This distinction applies to Islam as much as to any other ideological system that proclaims social equality as an ideal.

This distinction should not be entirely unfamiliar to us in India. As is well known, Indian society has been the most unequal society, the social inequality being institutionalised in the caste system. India's constitution went on to declare India to be a casteless and classless society. In so doing, the constitution was not proclaiming that social inequalities of the past had entirely disappeared and the society was egalitarian from the time it was promulgated. The only sensible way would be to recognise that, while social inequalities persist, the ideal that the Constitution provides is that of egalitarianism. This is also true of Islam. It proclaims social equality to be an ideal, but recognises social inequalities existing in society. By this token, there is no contradiction between Islamic support for an egalitarian society as a future goal and presence of caste or class differences as a social reality.

Social realities have a way of prevailing over sociological and theological formulations. Contrary to the argument of some sociologists and most theologians that caste does not exist among Muslims and untouchability is disallowed in Islam, the expression 'Dalit Muslims' has been finding increasing mention in the discourse of traditionally backward Muslim communities in recent years. However, there does not yet exist any clear understanding of what this expression actually means or which castes or groups it is supposed to denote. On the one hand, it has been used to denote a whole range of Muslim castes, which are currently included in the category of the Other Backward Classes. On the other hand, it has been used to denote those Muslim castes or groups, which converted from the 'untouchable' Hindu castes or are so severely stigmatised and are subjected to such extreme forms of social exclusion that would render them comparable to the Scheduled Castes.

The Mandal Commission compounded and reinforced this confusion. As is already well known, the Commission's task was to identify Other Backward Castes and to determine whether they should be eligible for reservation along the lines of the Scheduled Castes and Scheduled Tribes. There was no difficulty in this with respect to Hindu castes because administrative policy clearly recognised a distinction between Scheduled Castes and Other Backward Castes. Because the presidential order of 1950 clearly and arbitrarily laid down that 'No person who professes a religion different from the Hindu religion shall be deemed to be a member of a Scheduled Caste', the Mandal Commission lumped the severely stigmatised and extremely excluded among the Muslims with Muslim Other Backward Castes for purposes of affirmative action. Therefore, when the urgé for equality and social justice seized the imagination of the lowest social groups in other religious traditions and the word Dalit came to be seen as a short-cut carrier of that aspiration, the expression 'Dalit Muslims' came to be used for a wide variety of groups other than those severely stigmatised and excluded and on that ground comparable to Hindu 'ex-untouchable' castes for whom the term 'Scheduled Castes' was reserved.

One can arrive at an assessment of the extent of confusion that prevails at present with respect to the expression 'Dalit Muslims' by reading between the lines in the statements of those claiming to speak on their behalf as well as by considering the castes that they have been tempted to include under that category. N. Jamal Ansari writes: '…it is an established fact that Indian Muslim community is divided into castes and has a large deprived section. Before discussing constitutional provisions in respect of Dalits and exclusion of all 'Dalit Muslims' from those provisions, I think we must define "Dalit Muslims". Dalit means downtrodden, oppressed, suppressed and backward. Also, Dalit stands for untouchable and depressed classes. The term "Dalit" applies to members of those menial castes that have been graded lowly which they have inherited by accident of birth'. Likewise, Ali Anwar uses the words 'pasmanda' (meaning downtrodden and backward) and Dalit interchangeably and includes under 'Dalit Muslims' castes like Bhatiyara, Tikyafarosh, Itafarosh, Halalkhor, Khakrob, Mogalzada and Chirimar only some of which can be said to be severely stigmatized and excluded. In all such statements and lists, as their reading suggests, the expression 'Dalit Muslims' has been used as a generic term to denote all Muslim castes that are educationally and socially backward.

Clearly, there is need to define Dalit Muslims in more precise terms. Ansari suggested in his early work that the relationships between the ashraf and ajlaf on the one hand and the arzal on the other were shaped by considerations of social distance taking on the characteristics of untouchability. He mentioned that the members of the category called arzal were excluded both physically and socially. From a physical point of view, they tended to inhabit excluded localities and did not mix with the members of the other two categories. When it came to social intercourse, their relationship was characterized by strict maintenance of social distance and deference so that the members of the arzal communities had minimal and limited interaction with the members of the other communities. The expression should be restricted to refer to these castes alone. Since the expression 'Dalit' has come to acquire pejorative connotations, though it was originally used by the Dalit Panthers Movement as a short-hand way of referring to the extremely deprived and excluded castes, many Muslims may not like that expression to be used in the context of Muslim castes. Even so, there is need to recognise that the castes to whom we have here referred to as Dalit Muslims do form a class separate from the other categories of Muslim castes and need to be distinguished on account of the extreme degree of stigmatisation and exclusion suffered by them.

There is need for rich and focussed ethnographic research on such castes. This research should seek to understand the attitudes of the non-arzal castes and groups toward the members of the arzal category and to gauge the extent and intensity of discrimination suffered by them today. It is possible that with the introduction of sanitary toilets and other technological changes the arzal castes no longer engage in he demeaning and defiling occupation of scavenging but social distance from them continues to be maintained. It is also possible that the forms of discrimination and stigmatisation practised against the arzal castes have changed, but they may have taken other forms. Only focussed social research can indicate the contemporary situation of the arzal castes in contemporary Muslim society.

They were admitted to the house, but only for the performance of their services, in doing which they were required to ensure that they did not touch members of the household or other things that carried the risk of becoming polluted or rendered impure by their touch. They were asked to be present at social functions and festivals or on social occasions such as marriage or life cycle rituals, but this was not by virtue of any social right. It was by way of recompense for the service they rendered throughout the year. On all such occasions they sat some distance away from the main entrance for the guests and waited until everyone had been entertained to be given food that they were not supposed to eat then and there but carry it in the containers they brought with them to be eaten at home.

NOTES AND REFERENCES

1. See Gaus Ansari, *Muslim Castes in Uttar Pradesh*, (Lucknow, Ethnographic and Folk Culture Society, 1959).
2. Imtiaz Ahmad, 'Introduction', in Imtiaz Ahmad (ed.), *Caste and Social Stratification among Muslims*, Delhi, Manohar Book Service, 1973.
3. Charles Lindholm has argued that many of the features found in Muslim society are similar to those found among Muslims in other parts of South Asia and on that basis has argued that the Muslim social stratification found in India is an extension of the system found elsewhere (see Charles Lindholm, 'Paradigms of Society: A Critique of Theories of Caste among Indian Muslims', *European Journal of Sociology*, 1965, pp. 131-140). Many Muslims are themselves inclined to take a similar line of argument. This argument would have been tenable if Islamic scriptural sources had provided a blueprint of an Islamic

social stratification system. This not being the case, the argument fails to sustain itself. It is plausible that Islam did modify certain social practices including that of caste. Whatever practices were not sanctified by Islam but existed in India were attenuated. Whatever practices existing in India were in conformity with the Islamic ethos become more rigid. Thus, purdah practices, which already existed even in India, were rendered more rigid and strict and caste principles were relaxed or made less restrictive.

4. Nadeem Hasnian, in by H. S. Verma (ed.), *The OBCs and the Ruling Classes in India,* (Jaipur, Rawat Publications, 2005), pp. 84-97.
5. Husnain, p. 2.
6. Husnainm pp. 207-08.
7. Husnain, pp. 207-08.
8. Nazir, 1993: 2898.
9. Nazir, 2898.
10. *Census of India*, 1902, pp. 350-51.
11. Husnain, p. 208.
12. Pitirim A. Sorokin, *Social and Cultural Mobility,* (New York: The Free Press, 1959), pp. 13-14.

2

Minority Rights in the South Asian Countries with Special Reference to India

JAMES MASSEY

About the minority rights in South Asia, we need to remember three things: First, the countries of the South Asia have a unique context in the formation of their societal structures based on the social realities of their own, because in these countries the caste plays a major role. Second, the countries of South Asia have a large number of people belonging to dominant groups (majority), who have been expressing doubts regarding the validity of 'minority rights' as separate from the 'human rights'. Third, in most of the countries in the South Asia the minority rights are getting more and more pushed back, because of the increased role of the majoritarism along with the growing influence of' religious fundamentalism in the national politics. These points will be referred in our discussion of this paper, which has been arranged under the following sub-heads:

(i) Minorities: Who are they?
(ii) Minorities in the South Asian countries.
(iii) Minority rights and their relationship with human rights
(iv) A case of India

Minorities: Who are they?

Globally, the discussion on the issue of minorities and their rights in the present form has been going on now for almost a century. Immediately after the First World War from the time of the formation of the League of Nations, the concern of the minorities particularly in the context of Europe was on the agenda of the League of Nations. This is clear from a number of treaties that were sighned between 1919-23 among different European parties. These treaties were not only important for dealing with the immediate problem of the times in which these were made, but they also formed the basis for a positive understanding and response in future to the problem of minorities in general. In different forms, the discussion on the minority issue continues, but no formal attempt was made to define 'who is a minority'.

In 1945, after the League of Nations and the Second World War, the United Nations came into existence. The United Nations emphasis in general was more on the 'human rights' rather than on the 'minority Tights.' It is true that the United Nations' Charter extended its scope to encompass all human beings, but it did not make any reference to minorities. Therefore, even for a workable definition, we had to wait till the study report or Francesco Capotori, Special Rapporteur of the 'Sub-Commission on Prevention of, Discrimination and Protection of Minorities', on the Rights of Persons belonging to Ethnic, Religious mid Linguistic Minorities' (1977), which offered the following definition of a minority group':[1]

> "A group numerically inferior to the rest of the population of a State, on a non dominant position, whose members being national of the State-possess ethnic, religious or linguistic characteristics differing from those of the rest of the population and show if only implicitly, a sense of solidarity, directed towards preserving their culture, tradition, religion or language".

After the above proposal of definition, a revised version of the same was submitted to the Sub-Commission in 1985 by Canada's Jules Deschenes, which read as:[2]

> "A group of citizens of a State, constituting a numerical minority and in a non-dominant position in that State, endowed with ethnic, religious or linguistic characteristic which differ from those of the majority of the population, having a sense of solidarity with one another, motivated, if only implicitly, by a collective will to survive and whose aim is to achieve equality with the majority in fact and in law."

As can be seen even from the languages of the above two definitions, there is not much difference between these two definitions because both agree on the basic tests of a 'minority'. According to these two definitions – these tests include 'numerical inferior' and in a 'non-dominant position'. But a point to be noted here is that these tests are meant only for the 'nationals' or 'citizens'. Here 'refugees' or 'aliens' or 'migrant workers' are not covered by these definitions. This means that the groups like Korean in Japan will not be able to get a status of a minority on the basis of these definitions. Also, both the definitions refer to such groups, which though a minority, yet if they will not for some reasons press for their separate identity, offers a possibility of their being exploitated by the majority. This is exactly what has happened to the tribals and dalits in India. They have been forced to be included in the majority religion 'Hinduism', because this is the only way they can receive developmental help of the government's reservation policy.

The above-suggested definitions of 'minority groups' also do not explicitly bring out the criteria, which were used in the case of blacks of South Africa. Though they were a majority in number, yet they were considered a 'minority' in relation to a small white dominant community. Though the whites in number were small, yet they enjoyed political,economical and social power. On this basis a well-known Dalit leader Dr. B.R. Ambedkar demanded a minority status for the Dalits from the British during their rule, but the political leaders belonging to a majority religion including Mahatma Gandhi opposed this idea. Dr. Ambedkar's argument in favour of Dalits, getting a minority status was, "because a minority is weak, either in number, or because its social standing is low, or its educational standing is backward as compared with others, or because its economic strength is not sufficient to place it on a fighting par with other communities".[3] Here in this suggestion beside the numerical test, emphasis is also on the social, educational and economic strengths of a group, which can be considered a 'minority'. This possibly is the case and need of many countries of the South. Therefore, there is indeed a need for a comprehensive definition of a 'minority group' covering all the above criteria.

Minorities in the South Asian Countries

During the last three decades, I had the chance to visit number of Southern countries, which included: Ecuador, Brazil, Mexico,

Morocco, Kenya, South Africa, Malaysia, Zimbabwe, Uganda, Japan, South Korea, Taiwan, Philippines, Hong Kong, China, Thailand, Nepal, Bhutan, Sri Lanka, Myanmar, Singapore, Bangladesh, Indonesia, Malaysia, Cambodia, Australia, Jordan and Israel. In some of these countries, I had an opportunity to meet the minority groups openly, and in some cases I had to meet the underground groups quietly. Besides, the above countries of the South, I also had the chance to visit about a dozen countries of the North, which included the United States, Canada, United Kingdom, Germany, Netherlands, France and others. In these countries, I found the problems of the minorities are already on the rise (For example, U.K. and USA) and in other cases the problem has started coming up on the surface (For example, Germany).

Minorities in the South Asian Countries

During my visits to the above mentioned countries of the North and the South, one thing, which I observed, was that in the Northern countries the problem of the minorities and the question of the human rights violation is related more to the ethnocultural differences with the locals. Whereas in the Southern countries, it is centered around either on religious factor or on indigenous factor. This is especially true of Asia. For example, in India, Pakistan, Nepal, Bangladesh, Sri Lanka and Indonesia, these are religious minorities, which have been suffering at the hands of the majority religions.

But in number of countries, it is the indigenous people, who as minorities have to suffer at the hands of the dominant groups. Well-known examples are Australian Aborgines, Maoris of New Zealand, Ainus and Burakumin of Japan, Dalits and Tribals of India and various indigenous communities of the Philippines. The most serious problem of the indigenous groups in some of these countries is that countries like India, Bangladesh, Bhutan, Nepal are not even willing to recognize these communities as 'indigenous' and in this way their 'identity' is completely denied to them. In order to understand the case of the minorities, further, especially in South Asia, we will refer to six countries which include two countries with Muslims as a majority: Pakistan and Bangladesh; two with Buddhists as a majority: Bhutan and Sri Lanka; and two with Hindus as a majority: Nepal and India. The case of India, we will be discussing in detail.

1. Pakistan

In Pakistan, the basic discrimination faced by the minorities is on the question of 'religious freedom'. Though the late father of the nation Mr. Mohammad Ali Jinnah in his first address on August 11th, 1947 – at the time of the establishment of an independent State of' Pakistan made it very clear that he wanted Pakistan to become a secular State, in which all religions will enjoy the equal status. But the first Prime Minister in 1949, Nawabzada Liquat All Khan introduced an 'Objectives' resolution (inspite of the opposition from the non-Muslim religions) by which he proposed to make Pakistan a 'Muslim State'. This Objectives' resolution included one-of the following main clause: "where in the principle of democracy, freedom, equality, tolerance and social Justice as enunciated by Islam, shall be fully observed."[4]

The 'Objectives'resolution with the above clause was adopted in 1949 as the basis of Pakistan's Constitution. Though it envisaged a society based on the Quran, it assured the non-Muslims minorities to enjoy the complete freedom to "profess and practice their religion", through the following clause: "where in adequate provision shall be made for the minorities freely to profess and practice their religious and develop their culture."[5]

But at the time of the Prime Minister Zulfiqar Ali Bhutto in 1973, the 'Objectives' resolution was included in the Preamble of Pakistan in Constitution. Then in 1985, General Zia-ul-Haqu made the 'Objectives' resolution (through the 'Eight Constitutional Amendment') a substantial part of the Constitution as Article 2A, but he also got the word 'freely' removed from the above clause and by doing so he introduced a kind of 'religious apartheid'. To make the situation further complicated, now the Fifteenth Constitutional Amendment Bill based upon the Eighth Amendment, is on its way. If passed, the Prime Minister of the country will have extraordinary powers, who then will not be questioned by anybody or any institution including the Supreme Court of Pakistan. Secondly, it will introduce a possibility of the severest form of persecution of the religious minorities, which will go beyond the earlier holocausts of human history.[6]

The law related to the separate electorate (1985) is already into existence, which prohibits "the minorities from full-fledged democratic participation in the State politics."[7] We are already aware of the blasphemy law of Pakistan and its implication for the religious minorities. Because of this law in May 1998, Bishop John Joseph of Faislabad, was forced to take his own life and a number of young Christians like Ayub Masih and Salamat Masih had to suffer greatly. The story of the violation of the religious minorities rights is continuing to get longer every day in Pakistan.

2. *Bangladesh*

The story of Bangladesh with regards to the rights of the minorities, (though upto some extent is quite, yet no way it is different from Pakistan this sentence makes no sense) Bangladesh as a separate or independent nation came into existence in 1971. This new nation Bangladesh adopted the Constitution on November 4, 1972, which was fully secular in spirit. It prohibited all kinds of communalism, political use of religion including Islam by the State, discrimination on religion grounds etc. The Constitution stressed on the Bengali nationalism based on its language and culture. But then history of changes in the spirit of this Constitution started very quickly. To begin with the first head of the State, Sheikh Mujibur Rehman before his death, stressed in number of his speeches that efforts should be made to establish cordial relation with the Muslim countries. Later during the rule of General Zia-ur Rehman (1973 81), the principle of secularism more or less was dropped through various amendments in the Constitution. After General Rehman, during Mustaque Ahmed short rule (1975), Bangaladesh was made an "Islamic Republic of Bangladesh." Then General Irshad (1982-1990) introduced through an amendment of the Constitution "Bangladeshi Nationalism" which had an Islamic bias, in which Islam became a State religion. The present rulers are continuing with the same policy of Islamisation of the State. Number of laws has been passed such as the Vested Property Act, through which rights of the protection of the Hindus – taken away. In this process, how the minorities in Bangladesh are affected, Mr. Saleem Samad summed in these words:[8]

"It is evident that the true spirit and essence of democracy remains an illusion for the minorities in Bangladesh. In the name of majority rule, or democracy,they have been marginalised politically, economically as well as culturally ... The political parties and politicians in Bangladesh have used religion as a tool to consolidate their power base, and in the process have alienated the different minority groups."

3. *Bhutan*

I visited Bhutan towards the end the 1980s as part of a visiting team of the World Association for Christian Communication. This visit was unofficial in nature, but our main purpose was to observe in general the human rights situation and in particular the situation of the media. During our three days visit, we observed, how much a country can be closed with regard to the rights of its people. During our visit the issue of the Nepali Hindus was the main theme of discussion. Bhutan being a Buddhist country feels threatened by the presence of a large number of Nepali Hindus. We were also able to meet a very small community of Christians. On the surface, it looks as if Bhutanis a multi-religious society, but in reality it is limited to Buddhism alone and that too only to one denomination. The ethnic groups such as Nepali do not have the right to become citizens. Thousands of them are now living as refugees in Nepal and India.

In the case of Christians if they are non-Bhutanese, they can profess their religion, but cannot have a worship place of their own. The practice of Christianity for Bhutanese citizens is banned. During our visit, we were told that there are some converts and even a Roman Catholic priest, but he can only practice his Christian religion when he is in India.

Though Bhutan is a Buddhist country, it recognizes officially only one form of Buddhism, namely Dnikpa Kargyupa, as the state religion. Officially the State from the eighties has been pursuing a policy of converting all the minorities including Buddhists belonging to other orders to Drukpa Kargyupa Buddhism. The hegemonic policy is being followed very vigorously by the government, which threatens not only the rights of the various minorities, but their identities as well. Concerning the basic human rights including the rights of minorities, Narayan Katel's summary of negative human rights is noteworthy according to which, Bhutan does not have: freedom of speech and expression, freedom to peaceful assembly and union, right to justice, right to vote and free and fair election, freedom of religious, freedom of press and publication and printing, social and cultural rights etc.[9]

4. Sri Lanka

The problem of majority-minority in Sri Lanka is well described by a Sri Lankan free-lance writer Sammantha Weersooriya, in following the words: "While in Sri Lanka to-day, communal consciousness pervades all communities, it is the chauvinist ideology of the Sinhala Buddhist community, which is basic to the ideology and the current State and which today has become the psychological foundation for racist attitudes and behaviour of the part of majority Sinhala community." According to him, "This ideology's based on the myth that the Sinhala language speaking community is a 'pure' race descended from the Aryans, who inhabited Northern India 2,500 years ago. It is based on the mythology of a community of 'Aryan' who arrived in the Island about 500 B.C and became the first 'civilized' people to settle here. The fact that Buddhism was adopted by civilization as the State religion, very early, in the Island's history and has flourished here while it died out in its original birthplace of India has given rise to the belief of that this 'pure' Sinhala race has been, and yet is, the sole protector of Buddhism in its present form in the world."[10] Weersooriya in his discussion on Sinhala-Tamil (majority-minority) conflict adds:[11]

> "The propagation of the ideology was ably carried out through the education system of the Sangha, which willingly supported a State, which had gone as far as constitutionally guaranteeing the 'protection' of Buddhism. In this process it was the second largest ethnic group, the Tamil-speaking community, which felt the strength of its own identity enough to resent the mono-cultural outlook of the State and the growing socio-economic discrimination against the minorities."

The above assertions of Samartha Weersooriya make the following points clear:

(a) The ideology based upon the racial factor of majority being as Sinhala and the Buddhism as their religion (of majority) is the main reason behind to-day majority minority (Sinhala-Tamil) problem.

(b) The mythical belief Sinhala as "pure' race and part of the Aryan race is the other reason for the same problem.

(c) The State got support from the majority religious group

against the minority religious group in exchange, which the State gave the Constitutional protection to the religion of the majority (Buddhism) is the third reason for the current problem.

(d) The minorities specially the Hindu Tamil speaking group, who already got their own well established identify felt threatened from the above 'monocultural out- look' of the State to their identity, therefore their resentment.

(e) Because of the above reasons, minorities got discriminated both socially as well as economically.

5. Nepal

Technically speaking, Nepal is the only Hindu country in the world. Hinduism has been declared by the Constitution as the State religion. Nepali society is divided on caste basis. The upper caste include Bahuns, Chetris, Thakuris and Jaistis, who only had the right to wear sacred thread. But these upper castes are only 29 per cent of the total population. The remaining Nepali are considered as lower castes or untouchables. There are also many ethnic communities who fall in the categories of indigenous people. Dr. Krishen Bhattachan has done a very good analysis of the various majority minority communities divided on the basis of inter-caste, enter-ethnic and inter-religious. According to this analysis there are three level of conflicts:[12]

(a) The first conflict is between the dominant groups (Baliun-Clielhi), who form only 29 per cent of the total population and the remaining majority population. Because 70 to 90 per cent of key places in the State administration are controlled by the dominant group.

(b) The second conflict is between the hill people (again part of dominant group) and the non-hill. People, who in number are more, but they have been deprived the key positions in the administration later.

(c) The third level conflicts between the Hindu majority and minority religious (Muslims, Christians and Buddhist and others), who feel threatened by the attacks on their beliefs and practices by Hindu fundamentalism who draw support from the Nepal government directly or indirectly as part of the Hindu Kingdom.

Minority Rights and their Relationship with Human Rights

Historically, the 'human rights' were born out of the struggle oriented experiences of the people of the northern countries. The historical development of the human rights can be possibly divided into three stages, which covers a period of more than a century. The first stage begins with the bourgeois revolutions, particularly French and the American. One of the main points of this early stage was that the State should not impose any restriction on the sharing of the information. The second stage of human rights development took place within the socialist revolutions, during the first quarter of the 20th century in countries like Mexico and Russia. The main focus and emphasis during the second stage was on economic, social and cultural rights of the people and the state was supposed to assist in improving these. The third stage of the development of human rights began during the second quarter of the 20th century with the anti-colonialist revolutions, which stressed on national self-determination and non-discrimination.[13] Because of the historical relationship of human rights with these Northern countries' revolutions we find, the United Nations' Universal Declaration of Human Rights (1948) are more of individualistic in nature.

Internationally, the scope of the human rights is determined by the United Nations in its Charter Article I, which says these are "for all without distinction as to race, sex, language, or religion." For implementation in the same Article I of the Charter, international cooperation is sought which "implies that national borders put no limits to human rights, but that by their nature human rights represent trans boundary values."[14] Still inspite of all this Dr. Patrick Thomberry is right in his observation that the "minorities as such do not enjoy rights in the Declaration." Dr. Thornberry also observes that from the time of the Universal Declaration of Human Rights was promulgated, "the protection of minorities has been more or less absorbed into the wider concept of human rights."[15] But thanks to some of the later major instruments of international law, which actually has introduced a new system of human rights, recognizes the rights of the minorities. The best example of such instrument is the United Nations' Covenant on Civil and Political Rights' (1966), which in its Article 27 says: "In those states in which ethnic, religious or linguistic minorities exist persons belonging to such minorities shall not-be denied the right, in community with other members of their group, to enjoy their own culture, to profess and practice their own religion, or to use their own language."[16]

The other important international instruments, which focussed specially on the rights of minorities includes: Convention on the Prevention and Punishment of the Crime of Genocide (1948), International Convention on the Elimination of all forms of Intolerance and Discrimination Based on Religion or Belief (1981) and Declaration on the Rights of Persons belonging to National or Ethnic, Religious and Linguistic Minorities (1992). The Declaration of 1992 has cleared the earlier doubts and expanded the scope of minorities' rights. It very clearly states in its Article 1, which directs the member States concerning full protection of minorities, identity, which reads as: "1. States shall protect the existence and national or ethnic, cultural, religious and linguistic minorities within their respective territories, and shall encourage for the promotion of that Identity. 2. States shall adopt appropriate legislative and other measures to achieve those ends."[17]

The Article three (clause one) of the Declaration says: "Persons belonging to minorities in exercise their rights including those set forth in this Declaration individually as well as in community with other members of their group, without any discriminative have been accepted at the same time. Besides recognizing both of individual and collective rights, the Declaration of 1992 in Article 4, also has directed the member States about the protection of the human rights and fundamental freedoms of the minorities by saying. Persons belonging to minorities may exercise fully and effectively all their human rights and fundamental freedoms without any discrimination and full equality before the law." So as it stands today, 'minority rights' are enjoying a special status along with the human rights in general.

A Case of India

Till now whatever I have reflected upon, namely, on the relationship of human rights and minority rights, was the situation, which prevailed internationally for more than 40 years.

But why did it take the United Nations more than four decades to accept the reality of minorities, especially those belonging to the religious and linguistic minorities? It is because originally the human rights were the product of the historical context of the Northern countries, which have been far less pluralistic in nature. But—now as the reality of pluralism has entered their contexts—also, possibly the pressure of this reality has made this change easy.

On the other hand, the country like India which has been for centuries multi-religious, multi-linguistic, multi-cultural and multi-racial in nature, there was no hindrance to accept this reality right from the time of her independence. This is the reason why the Indian Constitution has fully accepted the principle of 'unity in diversity', or 'pluralism in togetherness.' About the close relationship between human rights and minority rights, this fact has been positively accepted in the Protection of Human Rights Act, 1993. This Act also deals with the constitution of a National Human Rights Commission according to which the Chairperson of the National Commission for Minorities is one of the ex-efficio members along with the Chairpersons of other two national commissions for the Scheduled Castes and Scheduled Tribes, and Women. The function of the National Human Rights Commission includes (besides some of the general) the following:[18]

(a) to intervene in any proceeding involving any allegation of violation of human rights pending before a court with the approval of such court;

(b) to visit, under intimation to the State Government, any jail or any other institution under the control of the State Government, where persons are detained or lodged for purposes of treatment, reformation or protection to study the living conditions of the inmates and make recommendations therein;

(c) to review the safeguards provided by or under the constitution or any law for the time being in force for the protection of human rights and recommend measures for the effective implementation;

(d) to review the factors, including acts of terrorism that inhabit the enjoyment of human rights and recommend appropriate remedial measures.

The reason why the Chairperson of the National Commission for Minorities has been made the ex-effiocio member of the National Human Rights Commission is because the Protection of Human

Rights Act 1993 expects from him or her to discharge his or her duty in carrying in such way that the human rights of the minorities are protected.

(a) Minority Rights and the Indian Constitution

Now what do we actually mean when we talk about the rights of the minorities? Are these rights different from human rights or the rights of the majority? Again to get a possible answer to these questions we will refer the case of India and her Constitution. (The Rights or Human Rights of the Minorities in the sense today we talk internationally, (particularly after the UN Declaration on the Rights of Persons Belonging to National or Ethnic, Religious and Linguistic Minorities in 1992), Indian Constitution already has taken care much of what the United National Declaration has spelled out in detail. Here it may be of help to refer to an analysis based report on 'new approaches to minority protection' of Asbajom Eide. Eide in his introductory statement to his suggested approaches says: "A human-right-based approach in pluralist societies must combine efforts to ensure equality in the common domain with acceptance of diversity in the separate domain. The separate domain is that reserved to the minority or its members to protect its identity as a group. The 'common domain' includes all other aspects of social life, which are subject to regulation, by the authorities."[19] The distinction between common domain and separate domain and their combination has been well kept and protected in the Indian Constitution.

The Constitution of India is very clear in its Preamble that the over all goal of India as a sovereign, socialist, secular, democratic Republic is "to secure to all its citizens: justice, social, economic and political; liberty or thought, expression, belief, faith and worship; equality of status and of opportunity, and to promote among them all fraternity assuring the individual and the unity and integrity of the Nation."[20] How will the country achieve this set goal? For this in the Constitution a provision has been made for the fundamental rights in Part III, which the State has to comply with. These are also judicially enforceable. But there is another set of rights stated in Part IV, which are connected with social and economic rights of the people. These rights are known as 'Directive Principles of State Policy', which legally are not binding upon the State, but are "fundamental in the governance of the country and it shall be the duty of the State to apply these principles in making laws". (Article 36). Then there is part IV A of the Constitution, which spells out the fundamental duties of the Indian citizens in which the reality of "the rich heritage of our composite culture" has been recognized fully.[21]

Indian Constitution has fully provided a definite space in the Constitution for both the domains, i.e. common as well as separate. In part III of the Constitution, which deals with the fundamentals rights, it has divided these rights very clearly into two parts, the rights, which fall, in the 'common domain' and the rights which go into the 'separate domain'. In the 'common domain', the following fundamental rights and freedoms are covered: the equality before the law (Article 14), prohibition of' discrimination on the ground of religion, race, caste, sex or place of birth article, equality of opportunity in matters of public employment (Article 16), protection of certain rights regarding speech, expression etc. (Article 19), protection in respect of conviction for offences (Article 20), protection of life and personal liberty (Article 2 1), protection against arrest and detention in certain cases (Article 22), prohibition of traffic in human beings and forced labour (Article 23), prohibition of employment of children in factories, etc. (Article 24), freedom of conscience and free profession, practice and propagation of religion (Article 25), freedom to manage religious affairs (Article 26), freedom as to payment. of taxes for promotion of any particular religion (Article 27), and freedom as to attendance at religious instruction or religious worship in certain educational institutions.

The above-mentioned rights are the fundamental or human rights and freedoms in the Indian Constitution are provided as part of the 'common domain'. (Most of these fundamental rights and freedoms have been listed in United Nations' Universal Declaration of Human Rights of 1948). On the other hand, there are two different kinds of minority rights, which fall in a 'separate domain' in the Indian Constitution. First such right is open to all the citizens, who form minorities in different parts of the country and the protection of their interests, are protected in Article 29, which reads as:[22]

***Article* 29**

1. Any section of the citizens residing in the territory of India or any part thereof, having distinct language, script or culture of its shall have the right to conserve the same.

2. No citizen shall be denied admission into any educational institution maintained by the State or received out of State funds on grounds only of religion, race, caste, language or any of them.

The Article 29 though provides the protection to the interests of minorities, yet it does not refer to the numerically less minorities. It actually refers to any section of the citizens, who may have a distinct language, script or culture even they may belong to majority community. For example, members of Hindu majority living in Punjab or Nagaland will have protection for their linguistic or cultural rights, where Sikhs and Christians are in majority respectively.

Next comes a very special fundamental right provided in Article 30 of our Constitution to the religious and linguistic minorities. This is also a part of the 'separate domain' provided to the minorities and their members to protect their identity. The text of this right reads as:[23]

1. All minorities, whether based on religion or language, shall have the right to establish and administer educational institutions of their choice.
2. The State shall not, in granting aid to educational institutions, discriminate against any educational institution on the ground that it is-under the management of a minority, whether based on religion or language.

This much about the Indian Constitutional position on the minority rights. What is interesting to note is that the Indian Constitution does not define the word 'minority'. The present definition on which the Indians are depending is given to them by the judiciary, according to which any community, which is numerically less, then 50 per cent of the population will be considered as 'minority group'.[24] At the national level basing itself more or less up on the same definition, the government of India has declared five religious groups as national minorities which includes: Muslims, Christians, Sikhs, Buddhists and Parsees. It is again the judiciary, which has spelled out the purpose of the rights of the minorities. These are to enable the minority to conserve and preserve their identity; to bring up their children in a congenial atmosphere, to bring about equality by ensuring the preservation of their institutions and to guarantee them these needed protections (in relation to Article

30).[25] Here one more point that needs to be remembered is that the Constitution of India does not give minorities any special rights, because these are the same, which are employed by the majority. Constitution offers only some safeguards to the rights of the minorities through Articles 29 and 30.

This much about the Indian Constitutional position on the minority rights. It becomes very clear now that in India the minorities do enjoy all the fundamental rights and freedoms, which have been offered to the citizens of India in general as well as the special rights, which Indian Constitution provides for them as safeguards. But there have always been doubts about the effective enforcement and implementation of these rights of minorities. Therefore, there arose a need for a special body to look into this concern of the minorities and in response to this need in January, 1978, the Government of India decided to set up an important body to be known as the "Minorities Commission." Then during 1992, the Parliament enacted the National Commission for Minorities Act 1992, changing the name of the Commission to "National Commission for Minorities" (NCM) and giving it a statutory status. The functions of the Commission along with its general functions included the following special functions:[26]

- *(a)* to evaluate the progress of the development of minorities under the Union and States;
- *(b)* monitor the working of the safeguards provided in the Constitution and in laws enacted by Parliament and the State Legislatures;
- *(c)* make recommendations for the effective implementation of safeguards for the protection of the interests of minorities by the Central Government or the State Governments;
- *(d)* look into specific complaints regarding deprivation of rights and safeguards of the minorities and take up such matters with the appropriate authorities.

The above Act of 1992 also gives the NCM special powers of a civil court in order to carry out the above functions.

(A) Violation of the Minority Rights in India

It is true that our Constitution of India has offered to all the citizens of the country the fundamental rights and freedoms (Articles 14-28) including the right to religious, freedom (Article 25). The Indian Constitution in real sense offers a balance between the national unity and with the cultural as well as social diversity. It is because those who framed the Indian Constitution knew that there would always be a tension between the majority and minority groups. Because majority always has the notion that the question of a separate identity of minorities will endanger the national unity and on the other hand, the minority groups also have a notion that if they will not be careful, the majority will absorb them and one day ultimately the majority will assimilate them. Strangely enough this tension during the second half of 20th century, instead of weakening has strengthened. The unfortunate incidents of 1997, 1998, 1999, 2000, and the later till now (on going recent attacks on religious minorities in Madhya Pradesh, Chattisgarh, Gujarat and Rajasthan) are a clear proof of this truth. Here some of these cases are listed in order to show the nature of the direct violation of the right of the minorities, particularly to religious freedom.[27]

1. A Christian priest was attacked and forced to walk naked for 8 k.m. in Dumka, Bihar on 2nd September, 1997.
2. Violation of religious right and police atrocities on Christian in Ludhiana, Punjab on 25th October, 1997.
3. Attacks on minorities (Christians and Muslims) in Gujarat. during July and August, 1998.
4. Gang rape of four Christian nuns in a Village Navapura, Dist. Jhabuva, Madhya Pradesh on 23rd September, 1998.
5. Attack on Christians, burning and demolishing of Church buildings in Dangs, Gujarat, during Christmas week, 1998.
6. The communal violence and attack on Muslim in Surathkal Dist. Manglore, December 29 - January 6, 1999.
7. Brutal burning to death of a Christian missionary Dr. Graham Steward Staines and his two soil in Manoharpur, Dist. Koenjhar, Orissa on 22nd January, 1999.
8. Burning of 157 Christian houses in Ranalai village, Dist. Gajapati, Orissa on March 16, 1999.
9. Burning of the Buddhist Monastery in Jaigaon, Dist. Jalpaiguri, West Bengal on 2nd June, 1999.

Here this list can be enlarged with the incident of violations that took place between 2001-06, but the space will not permit us to do so. Therefore, now I will deal with the most serious ongoing indirect violation of the rights of religious minorities.

(b) Indirect Violation

Beside the direct violation of minority religious rights, the Central government and some of the State governments have passed laws to restrict the religious freedom or minorities as well as of the Dalits. Here to make this point clear two sets of examples are discussed:

I. The Constitution (Scheduled Castes) Order, 1950.
II. The state Laws.

I. The Constitution (Scheduled Castes) Order, 1950

The Constitution (Scheduled Castes) Order, 1950 commonly known as 'Presidential Order 1950' is the first official order through which the first President specified the communities or groups to be included in the list of Scheduled Castes. The President was supposed to approve a list, who to be included in the most backward categories, so that the government may help them to develop. (For the purpose of the administration, a name for one of the historically backward groups used is 'Scheduled Caste'). But unfortunately, the President also fixed religion as a criterion according to which only those historically oppressed groups will be included in the list, who will profess Hindu religion. This is the reason the third paragraph, which followed the list of the Scheduled Castes read, as "Not withstanding anything contained in paragraph 2, no person who professes a religion different from Hindu, shall be denied to be member of a Scheduled Caste". This paragraph was amended by Parliament in 1956 to "Hindu or Sikh ' and in May 1990 to "Hindu or Sikh or Buddhist".

Here the point need to be noted is that the third paragraph of Presidential Order, 1950, contradicts directly with the first clause of Article 15 of our Constitution, which prohibits the State not to discriminate any citizen on grounds of religion and also Article 25, which gives to all citizens of the country "Freedom of Conscience". Besides these contradictions, this order also goes against the rights and safeguards provided to the larger sections of religious minorities (Muslims and Christians), having the Scheduled caste origin (Dalits). In fact, this restrict the fundamental rights as well as human rights of Dalits belonging to all religions include Hinduism. Because it does not allow them to change the religion according to their choice.[28]

II. The State Laws

The three states of Orissa, Madhya Pradesh and Arunachal Pradesh enacted laws in 1967, 1968 and 1978 respectively to control the conversion from one religion to other. These three state laws in their contents are identical and their purpose is also similar. The most recent laws related to the religious freedom were passed by the states of Tamil Nadu and Gujarat in 2002 and 2003 respectively (The state of Tamil Nadu later withdraw this law because of political reasons). The most recent law of similar nature has been passed by the state of Rajsthan in April, 2006. These are also to prohibit conversion from one religion to another by the use of force or inducement or by fraudulent means. The definition of 'conversion' according to these laws is 'renouncing one's religion and opting another'. The common prohibition clauses in all the above state laws are identical word by word, which reads as:[29]

"No person shall convert or attempt to convert, either directly or otherwise, any person from one religious faith to another by the use of force or by inducement or by any fraudulent means nor shall any person abet any such conversion."

In all the state laws, the expression "force", "fraud", "inducement" and "minor" are well defined. Here the meaning of word "inducement" we need to note specially, which in the text of Orissa Act, 1967, reads as follow: "Inducement shall include the offer of any gift or gratification either in cash or in kind and shall also include the grant of any benefit, either pecuniary or otherwise.[30] According to this definition of 'inducement, even the third paragraph of the 1950 Presidential Order can be also taken as a 'legal inducement' to Dalits, because they can get the status of Scheduled caste only if they stay in the boundaries of Hinduism or Sikhism or Buddhism.[31] If they change their religion to Islam or Christianity they loose the scheduled caste status as well as the benefits, which they will receive from the government.

The above State laws on the face value looks all right and the question related to the competence of enacting these laws already has been positively decided both by the High Court and Supreme Court. The court's final judgment was in favor of the States. But there are number of other questions, which one has to answer with regard to the scope and application of these State laws. For example, is the 'conversion' in these laws only relates to Christianity and Islam or it is also related to Hinduism, Sikhism, Buddhism and others. Is Hindu or Arya Samajists Sudhi Karan (re-conversion) is also covered by these laws. If yes, then, has anytime these have been applied against such actions of Hindu preachers. The answer is "no".

Besides the above serious discriminatory elements of all the state laws, the law of Gujarat has added more strict and enhanced punishments for those who will be proved offenders under these laws. This State law has put legal restriction by increasing the fine and punishment in the case of the conversion of the Schedules Castes (Dalits) and Scheduled Tribes (tribal). For example, the laws of Orissa, Madhya Pradesh and Arunachal Pradesh for the offenders, the punishment prescribed is imprisonment up to two years and fine up to Rs. 10,000/-. But in the case of Gujarat law, the punishment is increased to four years and fine up to Rs. 1,00,000/-. The same way in the law of Gujarat, the punishment for contravention of provisions of section, which has being quoted above, the fine has been increased from Rs.5,000/- to Rs.50,000/- and imprisonment from one year to three years.

Besides the above differences in the state laws related to religious freedom, Gujarat has added a clause 5, which has imposed a still more severe legal restriction on this right of the Indian citizens. This clause is related to the issue of prior permission, which to be taken from the District Magistrate with respect to conversion and it reads as follows: [32]

1. "Whoever converts any person from one religion to another whether by performing any ceremony by himself for such conversion as a religious priest to take part directly or indirectly in such ceremony shall take prior permission for such proposed conversion from the District Magistrate concerned by applying in such form as many be prescribed by rules."
2. "The person who is converted shall send an intimation to the District Magistrate of the District concerned in which the ceremony has taken place or the fact of such conversion within such period and in such form as may be prescribed by rules."

As mentioned above, there could not have been any problem if these laws could have applied equally to all the followers of all religion, but it is a well known fact that these are actually directed toward some of the minority religions specially Christianity and Islam. This is where the legal credibility of these laws becomes questionable. Also these laws in their implications are direct violation of the fundamental rights given to all the citizens in Articles 14 and 15 of the Indian Constitution.

Our above point will become further clear, if we look to the recent happenings in Gujarat concerning the Christians and Muslims and the result of which the 'Gujarat Freedom of Religious Act, 2003' has been enacted in order to curb basically the Christian right of 'propagation', which at the time of framing Article 25 of the Constitution, was accepted 'a fundamental part of Christian tenants'. Also, at the time the practice of *Shidhii Karan* (re-conversion) of Hindu religion and Christian baptism were equated.[33] But as it is again a well known fact that on regular basis a number of Dalits and tribals are made to go through the practice Shudhi Karan in the name of 'homecoming', but no actions ever has been taken against such happenings. It is here one has to demand the equality before the law specially while implementing the above mentioned laws created by the states related to the 'Freedom of Religion' in our country. But why these violations? A brief answer is offered here.

I. Reason for the Violation

The major reasons for the growing violation of the rights or the minorities in India are listed here:

1. Both at the central as well as states levels there is absence of 'political will' either to implement the various safeguards provided in the Indian Constitution for the protection of the rights of the minorities or even to protect these safeguards.
2. During last fifty-six years from the time of the Indian Constitution adopted, very rare individuals or group culprits involving in the action leading to the violation of minority rights are punished. This is one of the main reasons either in the increase of the cases of the violation of the minority rights or the continuing of these violations.
3. The ideological foundations of the states that promoted and

maintained ethnic, linguistic or religious superiority of the majority groups.
4. Unitary political structures and a form of majoritarian democracy that effectively blocked the legitimate participation of the minorities in the decision making process.
5. The communalization of politics and politicization of religions that kept the minorities out of the mainstream, and the repressive and the discriminatory laws and practices against the minorities of some of the states.
6. A lack of awareness among the minorities about their human rights and democracy without which it was difficult for minorities to fight for their rights.
7. The conflicts of interests among the minority communities, a product of denial of equitable access to social, economic and natural resources, often hindering the emergence of a united front of minorities.
8. And lastly, the so-called mainstream ideology of assimilation reinforced by the education system, which promoted hegemonism and political and social level and contributed to the alienation of the minorities from the larger society.

II. Concluding Remarks

Finally, I want to close the discussion of this paper by stressing a point that the Indian Constitution with regard to the religious minorities offers a best model in the world. But certainly there is a need of a full social commitment and political will to implement the same. But, besides the social commitment and political will, which need to be created at the political levels, the other level needs encouragement to make efforts to enhance the religious solidarity among the followers, of all living faiths (religions). This solidarity is already a living reality in our country, which actually is the staying power of our multi-faith, multi-ethnicity, multi-language and multi-cultural context. It is here a definite role of, all of us as part of the civil society become pertinent, which can help in removing the discrimination and stopping the on going violations of the rights of religious minorities and the dalits. This we can do by entering into the process of advocating the rights of Dalits and Minorities.

NOTES AND REFERENCES

1 Francesco Capotari, *Study on the Rights of Persons belonging to Ethnic, Religious and Linguistic Minorities*, United Nation, New York, 1991, p. 96 (pars 568).

2 Patrick Thornberry, *Minorities and Human Rights Law*, the Minority Rights Group, London, 1991, p. 7.

3 Vasant Moon (ed.), *Dr. Babasaheb Ambedkar: Writings and Speeches*, Vol. 2, Government of Maharashtra, Mumbai, 1992, p. 533.

4 Sumanta Banerjee (ed.), *Shrinking Space: Minority Rights in South Asia*, Lalitpur, Nepal, 1999, p. 141.

5 Cecil Chaudhary, "The Fifteenth Constitution Amendment Bill: An Analysis" in Sumanta Banerjee, (ed.) *op. cit.*, p. 142.

6 *Ibid.* pp. 137-42.

7 Khalid Ahmed, "Pakistan - Violation of the Rights of the Minorities in Pakistan" in Sumanta Banerjee (ed.), *op. cit.*, p. 122.

8 Saleen Samad, "Sate of Minorities in Bangladesh", in Sumanta Banerjee (ed.), *op. cit.*, p. 94.

9 Narayan Katel, "Minority Rights in Bhutan", in Sumanta Banerjee (ed.), *op. cit.*, p. 22.

10 Weerasooriya, Sammuntha Weerasooriya, *Minorities in Sri Lanka - the Bourgeoisie Divide and Rules in 'The Image of God in Minorities'* Edited by Ahu Jaewoong, Hong Kong, 1984, p. 7.

11 *Ibid.*, p. 9.

12 Krishna B. Bhattachan, *Minority Rights in Predatory Nepalese State in 'Shrinking Space: Minority Rights in South Asia, op. cit*, pp. 45-46.

13 *Media Development*: Journal of the World Association for Christian Communities, London, No. 4, 1988, Vol. XXXV, p. 1.

14 *Manuel on Human Rights* Reporting under six major Inter-national Human Rights instruments, United Nations, Geneva 1997, pp. 4-5.

15 Patrick Thornberry, *op. cit.*, p. 11.

16 Iqbal A. Ansari (ed.), *Readings on Minorities - Perspectives and Documents*, Vol. 1, Now Delhi, 1996, p. 220.

17 *Ibid.*, p. 311.

18 *Ibid.*, Vol. 2, pp. 508, 512-513.

19 Asbjorn Eide, *New Approaches to Minority Protection*, Minority Right Group, London, 1991, p. 12.

20. *The Constitution of India* (as on Ist June 1996) Government of India, New Delhi, 1996, prelimns.
21. *Ibid.*, pp. 5-9.
22. *Ibid.*, p. 9.
23. *Ibid.*
24. James Massey, *Minorities in a Democracy -The Indian experience*, Manohar Publication, New Delhi, 1999, p. 41.
25. *Ibid.*, pp. 42-43.
26. *Minorities India*, Newsletter of National Commission for Minorities, Vol. I : No. 1, Spring 1997, p. 4.
27. James Massey, *Rights of Minorities to Religious Freedom* (under Article 25), (A study report), National Commission for Minorities, New Delhi, 1999, pp. 32-33.
28. *Ibid.*, pp. 42, 48, 50.
29. *Ibid.*, p. 42.
30. James Massey, *Rights of the Minorities to Establish & Administer Educational Institutions* (under Article 30 of the Constitution), (A study report), National Commission for Minorities, New Delhi, 1998, pp. 55-58.
31. Tahir Mahmood, "Islamic Law and State Legislation on Religious Freedom and Conversion in India", in *Contemporary Studies*, Part II, p. 178.
32. *Gujarat Freedom of Rights Act, 2003*, clause No. 5, page 3.
33. *Constituent Assembly Debates*, Vol. 7, p. 836.

3

Articulation of Self and the Other: Emergence of the Dalit Movement in Andhra Pradesh

A. SATYANARAYANA

In this essay I will focus on the historical context and the nature of dalit assertion, identity and consciousness in modern Andhra during the pre and post-independence period.[1] It examines the growth of dalit consciousness and literary works of some dalit intellectuals that reflected the agony and anger of dalit masses. An attempt is also made to analyse the nature of dalit mobilization and of literary representation of dalit sensibilities and the emergence of dalit awareness in the writings of selected dalit writers. Indeed, the emergence of dalit autonomous movement and dalit literary texts viz., poems, drama, novel, short-stories, essays, etc., were related to the specific socio-political upheaval in colonial Andhra which was characterized by the growing social reform and non-brahmin movements as well as constitutional reforms and dalits' urge for representation in political/administrative institutions.

Dalit Assertion During Colonial Period

The formation of Adi-Andhra Mahasabha in 1917 signified the collective self-mobilization of dalits for self-respect, dignity, equality and social justice. This movement also heralded the new found identity, unity and solidarity among the dalit communities, for it articulated their resolve to escape the ascriptive and hereditary fixation of occupation and formalized their struggle to democratize the civil society and appropriate emerging new forms of power structures. Three factors contributed for the development of social radicalism among dalits in colonial Andhra: *(a)* influence of pre-colonial anti-brahmanical heterodox sects (vaisnavism, saivism, nasraiah etc.) and spread of Christianity; *(b)* upper caste-led social reform movements like Arya Samaj and Brahma Samaj; and *(c)* the growth of Western education.[2] Consequently, a host of the dalit organic intellectuals through their writings launched an attack on the Brahmanical ideology and thus became the facilitators in critiquing and undermining the unequal social order and social inequality based on caste and birth. In particular, I propose to focus on the following dalit intellectuals and activists.

Bhagya Reddi Varma

Bhagya Reddi Varma, alias Madari Bhagaiah, (1888-1939) (Redu=Reddi; Varma=title) founder of Dalit movement in modern Andhra in the first decade of twentieth century.[3] First President of Adi-Andhra Mahasabha in 1917, he was also the founder of Adi-Hindu Social Service League and Adi-Hindu Bhavan in Hyderabad for "removing ignoble appellations" and spreading the Adi-Hindu identity and education among lower castes. He rejected the panchama identity and organized many Adi-Hindu conferences to spread awareness among the dalit communities. He asserted that the so-called untouchables were never a part of caste-Hindu (Aryan) society. He suggested a break from orthodox Hindu tradition and religion as the primary necessity for ending the plight of dalits as well as to maintain their separate identity. As the foremost champion of dalit cause he started a paper called *Bhagyanagar Patrika*, a Telugu fortnightly devoted for dalit upliftment in the Nizam's state. Later in 1937 the same was brought out under the title *Adi-Hindu*, edited and published by him. He described Adi-Hindus as descendants of the original inhabitants of this country who were rulers and owners of this land of their birth before the advent of the Aryans to the country. About the anti-caste radicalism of Bhagya Reddi Varma and his negation of brahmanical tradition, Gail Omvedt remarked: "In treating untouchables as the original 'sons of the soil', in seeing Brahmans as outsiders pushing all the original Indians down to south India, he was said to have used the term 'Adi-Hindu' in a way in which 'Hindu' did not refer to religion but was by foreigners to those living in India".[4]

Gurram Jashuva

Gurram Jashuva (1895-1971)–titles Mahakavi, Kavi-Chakravarti. He was the author of *Gabbilam* (The Bat) a Long poem, 1941 and *Anadha* (The Orphan), 1940. He questioned the very creation of the fifth order, the Panchama varna; he also questioned the wisdom of the caste Hindus in treating the Dalit masses as Panchamas. He wrote:[5]

We heard that for the old Brahma
Born four sons
The wretched lower than the animal who is this
Fifth caste person! Savitri!! (O' Mother).

In *Bat,* Jashuva portrays the miserable conditions of the dalit masses.

When his (dalit's) hands do not work
The green fields hesitate to yield crops
His sweat, provides food for the world
But he himself has no food.

He also reflects how the poisonous snake called Hinduism perpetrates oppression on dalits:

By swallowing the blood of the wretched (dalit)
Lives the iron ankleted Mother
Upon smelling his air hisses with vengeance
The four-hood Hindu cobra.

Gurram Jashuva is remembered as a forceful poet who raised strong voice of protest in verse against the caste system, untouchability and socio-economic inequalities. He inaugurated a new era in modern poetry by taking up the problems of dalit literature. He was a source of inspiration for many young dalit youth and writers.

Kusuma Dharmanna

Kusuma Dharmanna (1896-1948) was one of the prominent Dalit organic intellectual leaders of the Adi-Andhra movement, a famous poet, 'Kavi Veera' and a prolific writer. His famous writings include *Madya Paana Nishedamu* (1930); *Nalla Dora Thanam* (1933); *Harijana Satakamu* (1933).[6] He is also called as the forerunner of Dalit movement in Andhra. He was considered a basic poet, a gifted speaker and an able leader. To awaken the dalit masses to fight for their civil and democratic rights he founded a weekly called *Jayabheri*. He was very critical of Brahmanical ideology and critiqued the *varna* system in his various writings. His poetry depicts the multiple dimensions of exploitation of dalit masses by the rich peasantry and also the sorrow and anger of dalit labourers. Kusuma Dharmanna denounced caste Hindus for the inhuman practice of untouchability.[7]

They consider us inferior to dogs and foxes
Sit beside a leprosy patient
Domesticate dogs and monkeys with affection
Love cats and birds
Don't trouble pigs
Allow crows to touch water
But abuse us and don't allow us to approach them.

His poetry was indeed "the true representation of unfolding contemporary social reality".

Jala Ranga Swamy

Jala Ranga Swamy(1904b) born at Kambala Peta in Rjahmundry. He was a teacher by profession and worked for Dalit education; he established many educational institutions along with his wife Jala Mangamma. His writings include *Antarani Vaarevaru?* (Who are the Untouchables?) (1930); *Malasuddhi* (cleanliness of Malas) (1930). In his long poem *Antaranivarevaru* he claimed social equality by claiming glorious ancestry. He wrote:[8]

The great warriors of Puranas were our people
Vasistha, Valmiki belonged to our dynasty
Veda Vyasa, Parasara were our people
Hanuman, Sugreeva were our brothers
Did not great mothers of heroes born amongst us?
Did not they observe chastity?
Is not Arundhati, the daughter of our caste?
Sabari, Matangi were our women
A caste in which such great people were born being alienated
We were made lowly people, excommunicated.

Rangaswamy along with his wife also established *Adi-Jana Grandha Mandali* and published about 12 works. Important among them are *Dunnevadide Bhumi* (land to the tiller). The first Telugu Dalit novel *Ryotu Pilla* (peasant girl) was written by his wife Jala Mangamma (1909-1974). She also started a paper Veerabharati in 1935.[9]

Nakka China Venkaiah

Nakka China Venkaiah, (1892-1970)–the most famous among his writings are Harijana Keertanalu, (1935). He was born on 4 January 1892 at Mummidi Varam-Sivaru Palli Palem in Amalapuram taluk, East Godavari district. He was a teacher-manager at Kumana Palli (1909), later appointed as a teacher in an Adi-Andhra school at Mummadi Varam. He had close connections with the non-Brahmin leadership of the Justice Party and movement. He encouraged a lot of Dalit youth to join the movement, including, Pamu Rama Murthy and Eeli Vada Palli. He was a member of the executive council of the East Godavari Adi-Andhra Mahajana Sabha from 1937 to 1942.[10]

Boyi Bheemanna

Boyi Bheemanna (1911-2005) was a legend of the Dalit intellectuals. He graduated (1936) from P.R. College, Kakinada and completed his B.Ed. at Rajahmundry (1937), was an associate editor for a Dalit journal *Jayabheri*. He published nearly 50 works including *Paaleru* (a farm boy) (1940), *Kooli Raju* (the labour king) (1947), *Jaana Paduni Jabulu* (1940), *Ragavashistam* and many more. In his poetry, Bheemanna pleaded for social equality.[11]

> Around the neck of the powerful Indian nation
> Caste, religion are the hangman's ropes
> Destroy the guile of caste and religion
> Eradicate the human inequalities.

B.S. Murthy

B.S. Murthy (b1906) is the best example of the emergence of Dalit political articulation and mobilization.[12] He was educated at Rajahmundry and at Madras, elected secretary of Andhra Pradesh Harijan Sevek Sangh from 1940-49, elected member of the Madras Legislative Assembly in 1937 and the Minister of Industries and Labour; later became Deputy Minister in Nehru's cabinet. He also took part in national movement. He established a paper called Navajeevna (new life). He has been a catalyst in causing socio-economic mobility among dalits during the early decades of independence. As a political activist he took positive steps for the spread of education and employment and advancement among dalit youth.

In addition to above literary works, the emergence of dalit journals in the 1930s played a significant role in creating awareness among dalit masses. They articulated and highlighted dalit issues and kindled their consciousness. The main periodicals include *Jayabheri* of Kusuma Dharmanna, *Adi-Andhra* of Didla Pullayya, *Veera Bharathi* of Jala Ranga Swamy, *Navajeevana* of B.S. Murthy, *Harijana* of Vundru Subba Rao and the *Jeevana Jyothi* of Chuttumalla Venkata Ratnam. The writings of Dalit intelligentsia played a major role in bringing about unity and a feeling of oneness, and self-respect. They helped to establish an egalitarian society and create a vision for the future.

Dalit feminist writing also became a part of Adi-Andhra movement. The example of Jala Mangamma (1909) is quite interesting. Along with her husband, Jala Ranga Swamy she worked for dalit upliftment and contributed for dalit literature. Influenced by Gandhian nationalist thought, she worked as a teacher and taught in the night schools. She established Harijana Mahila Sangam and fought against untouchability. She also established hostels for dalit girls during 1928-31. She authored few novels and edited a paper. In her works, she dealt with the realities of caste dynamism of patriarchy and the peculiarities of dalit women's oppression. Her writings also explore the elementary aspects of dalit feminism.

Dalit intelligentsia had good knowledge of the insight into the life experiences of the masses about whose problems they wrote: their thoughts and feelings were fused with those of the masses. The subject matter for their works was provided by the everyday life experience and existential problems of the dalit masses. These writers, who found inexhaustible raw material in the society and community in which the masses were born, shaped it into a realistic literary representation. The main characteristic feature of dalit literature was its contemporaneity and realistic presentation. The savarna scholars who depicted dalit problems in their writings were guided neither by the philosophical and ideological tradition of the bhakti saint-poets nor by the liberation ideology and philosophy of Phule and Ambedkar. The dalit scholars critiqued the brahmanical social order as well as untouchability. In this sense it can be said that the dalit intellectuals of the pre-independence period were the forerunners to the contemporary dalit literary and cultural movements in the state. The distinctiveness in Dalit literature lay in the fact that there are certain ideas that were intrinsic to Dalit literature. The foremost realities that they propound are self-respect, the ideal of humanism, equality, and liberty. Those were some of the important facts regarding Dalit literature and Dalit writings as an instrument of liberation. Throughout history they have been searching for their roots and trying to create unity among themselves that is why, for them, generating history or writing literature is a self-liberating process. Dalit intellectual assertion contested the dominant brahmanical narratives and perceptions of their untouchable identity by emphasizing the purity and distinctiveness of their lives and demanding social equality. The writing of Bhagya Reddi Varma and Boyi Bheemanna are particularly note worthy in this regard.

However, Dalit intellectuals did not accept their exclusion. A Dalit Telugu poet who wrote a long poem called '*Gabbilam*', the 'Bat' (Chamgadar in Hindi) in which he narrated the oppressive social conditions of Dalit rejected the rationale of untouchability. He cautioned the Dalits not to go to the priests and let their words be heard by them but to address their words directly to God. The poet accepted that the Dalits were outside the social organization and now they wanted to be a part of it and to be included in the larger social organization. The Dalit communities of Andhra Pradesh refused to be addressed as Panchamas, Depressed Castes, Outcastes etc., by the first decade of the twentieth century. They resisted the usage of such terminologies attributed to them. Claiming themselves to be the original inhabitants of this land, they began calling themselves as 'Adi-Andhras'. The awareness among the Dalits for asserting their demands for equality was noticed as early as 1920's. Dalit literature was produced in Andhra particularly from 1930's onwards and this was also the time when the Gandhian liberation movement for Dalits had started. However, the majority of Dalits rejected being called as 'Harijan', the name conferred to them by Gandhi. Therefore, majority of the Adi-Andhra movement activists followed the ideology of Dr. Ambedkar rather Gandhi. Kusuma Dharmanna, a popular Dalit poet played an important role in popularizing further the ideals of Dr. Ambedkar through his popular booklets of long poems, short stories and essays. With the help of these literatures, he propagated an alternative vision and an alternative view of history. In one of his poems, he mentioned that unless the social oppression was eradicated, there could not be freedom in the post-independence period.

From Adi-Andhras to Dalits: Dalit Articulation in Post-Independence Period

In recent years growing incidents of murder, arson, rape etc., perpetrated against dalit masses by the dominant upper castes indicated a complex and diverse pattern.[13] Yet, one this is clear viz., the increasing assertion and awakening among dalits about their rights and quest for equality has become intolerable to the upper castes. The formation of Adi-Andhra Mahasabha (1917) and the Dalit Mahasabha (1985) are the two important landmarks in the history of dalit liberation in modern Andhra. The issues raised by these movements pertaining to self respect, democratization of civil and political society and emancipation continued to pose a serious challenge to the post-colonial state in India. As is well-known that instead of resolving the problem of caste discrimination and oppression, untouchability and caste violence the political leadership of this country is subverting the constitutional and administrative apparatus. In Andhra Pradesh upper caste atrocities against dalits were intensified on the eve of independence and - formation of Indian Republic. Let us examine the socio political context and the social roots of violence during post-independence period. Though perpetuation of upper caste violence against dalits in rural Andhra is not a new phenomenon, its extent and intensity began to grow since the 1950s. The climax of caste conflict was witnessed by the ghastly massacre of dalits in Karamchedu (1985) and Chunduru (1991). Let me briefly list the incidents of upper caste violence against dalits in Andhra Pradesh.

Pre-Karamchedu (1985) Upper Caste Violence Against Dalits[14]

Sl.No.	*Place of Incident*	*Reason and Nature of Incident*
1.	Haribanda and Makannepuram 1950 (Vishakhapatnam dist.)	Dalits drew water from common well on 'Harijan Day'
2.	Appikatla, 1950 (Guntur dist.)	Agriculture labour demanded wage rise

(Contd.)

Sl.No.	Place of Incident	Reason and Nature of Incident
3.	Kasukurru	Dalit couple (Doctor) went in a marriage procession through main street in a car
4.	Kalvacherla	A Dalit woman was tortured for drinking water from a public well.
5.	Sambararam (Kurnool dist.)	Caste Hindus objected to the construction of a community hall in the dalit locality, which was close to a public pathway. In the attack, a dalit was killed and a couple of haystacks were burnt.
6.	Govindpet (Nizamabad dist.)	A Dalit woman was beaten for suspected robbery.
7.	East Godavari	One Dalit was killed and six other brutally attacked when they wanted to enter into a temple.
8.	Atmakur	A Dalit boy beaten to death on suspicion of theft.
9.	Nikkakuru (Krishna dist.)	Two dalit youth were tortured to death on suspicion of theft.
10.	Ramanna Palli	Dalits were beaten and their locality was burnt, because they refused to work for low wages and demanded increase.
11.	China-Ogirala (Krishna dist.)	One dalit was murdered and 20 injured because the government granted wastelands to them.
12.	Kanchikacharla (Krishna dist.)	One dalit was burnt to death on suspicion of theft and was roasted alive.

The Ilay Perumal Committee (1969) and the sample survey in 1975 revealed that in rural Andhra caste discrimination was rampant. Two glass system in hotels/teashops have been quite common. The dominant upper castes, as landowners and employers of labourers, thus exerted considerable power over the dalits. In the villages majority of dalit agricultural labourers and poor peasants/ tenants were dependent upon the rich Kamma, Kapu and Reddy peasantry. Whenever the class demands like wage increase were articulated by dalit communities, they are subjected to caste oppression like social boycott and denial of access to village economic resources. The dominant rich peasantry also did not tolerate any upward mobility among the dalits. Whenever dalit families acquired some wasteland, whose-sites and other land grants from government the caste Hindu rich peasantry subjected them to physical attacks. The struggle for wage increase and land distribution by dalits resulted in retaliation from the dominant caste peasantry in the form of abuse, harassment, molestation of women and destruction of property. Dalits became easy target for trivial accusations of theft and witchcraft. There was no dearth of instances of caste discrimination in terms of preventing their entry into temples, taking drinking water from public wells and tanks, denial of common cups in the teashops, etc. The perpetuation of violence against dalits by the upper castes is closely related to the socio-economic and political domination of the rich peasantry in the countryside. The growing assertion of dalits for the actualization of the concept of citizenship, mass literacy as the basis of new civil life and the social/spatial mobility as new principle of social life invited victimization by the dominant caste peasantry. The concern of them for social mobility, education and diversification of occupation was consciously negated by the dominant castes. The unabated caste violence against dalits in the Andhra countryside is a clear proof of this.

The Dalits of today has moved to the center-stage and unlike in the past they could not be taken for granted. They were creating new identities both in civil and political society and in such changing circumstances they had become more assertive and were demanding freedom and equality from the society. For the Dalits freedom meant equality, according to a Telugu poet, equality is freedom. Dalits had started organizing themselves and had formed associations, way back in 1890's long before Gandhiji started campaigning for their uplift in 1932. Unfortunately, despite efforts made by both Dalit and non-Dalit groups to bring them into the mainstream, instances of atrocities on them, whether big or small, are going on unabated.

In the 1980's, the Adi-Andhras began to associate themselves with the term 'Dalit'. Dalit Mahasabha was formed in 1985 after a cruel incident took place in which six Dalits were butchered, as they demanded access to public wells and village tanks.[15] An upper caste person objected to Dalits women washing clothes at the public tank. When she resisted, the entire Dalit area was attacked in which six Dalits youth were murdered. In 1991, another incident took place in which a Dalit youth went to a cinema hall and purchased an upper class ticket. While sitting, his leg accidentally touched the body of an upper caste boy. He was given a sound thrashing by the upper caste. The incident sparked off a series of events that led to the butchering of another 21 Dalits. Thus these kinds of oppression gave rise to a new kind of awareness among Dalits that was not seen earlier. From untouchable to Harijans, to Adi-Andhras, and then to Dalits, they formed different identities at different phases of history. Today an alternative history has emerged which has been rejected by the mainstream historians. In the mainstream history, the heroes of Dalit communities were depicted as bandits or dacoits. In retaliation, the Dalits have now started asserting themselves by rewriting their own history and providing to the world that they were rulers at one point of time in history. This period is also witnessing the emergence of various revolutionary ideas that is paving the way for various movements such as the Naxalite movement, which was essentially a Dalit movement, as 90% of the Naxalites were either Dalits or from Bahujan lower caste/ communities. All this is an indication of their increased assertiveness. Due to the growing social movement, the literature, too, has moved to different context. The Dalits of today are not ready to accept sympathy. They want to express themselves freely to articulate their own vision. In the post-1980s period in modern Andhra especially "dalit identity indeed became the foundation for the formation of a new politics, raising a new set of issues and mobilizing all dalit castes collectively under a single umbrella. The core issue of refashioning a pure, 'untouched' identity remained, but most significant contribution of this new politics [and articulation] lay in the emergence of a dalit identity as a foundational category for social and political organization of knowledge, lives and agendas".[16]

Today the Dalits are questioning the politics of silence. They are questioning how it is that hardly anything has been said or written in the mainstream literature or in the history about Dalit culture and literature. They question and reject narratives and categories constructed by the upper caste Hindus. It has not only meant to contest the dominance of upper caste authority but also to question and reject the notions of purity and pollution attached to them, their identity, history and culture by the upper castes. The dalit intellectuals ask why has no cognizance been taken of the emerging consciousness in their community? It is precisely to prove their resistance and to sensitize the Dalit community that the Dalits have created their own literature, which is humanistic; it is about self-reliance, and self-confidence. Even today Dalits are talking in terms of democratic participation. They want to make a formal democracy a real democracy. This is the kind of urge that is growing among the community and the facts need to be recorded and documented in this direction.

Incidents of Violence against Dalit by Caste Hindus in Post-karamchendu Period (1985-1991)[17]

Sl.No.	*Place of Occurrence*	*Nature of the Incident*
1.	Karamchendu (Prakasham, dist.)	Six Dalits killed and three Dalits women raped in a mass assault by hundreds of forward caste men of the Kammam caste. A politically active son-in-law of the then chief minister, N.T. Rama Rao belongs to this village.
2.	Hasnapur (Adilabad, dist.)	Reddy landlords closely related to the MLA, Adilabad, killed two youth of the dhobi and barbar castes for refusal to procure a prostitute on their demand
3.	Neerukonda (Guntur, dist.)	One elderly dalit murdered in mob attack by the Kamma community, close relatives of the then Health Minister in the Andhra Pradesh Government.
4.	Gudivada (Vizianagaram, dist.)	One dalit labourer killed in a dispute over a small patch of tank-bed land by a mob of backward caste farmers led by Raju caste (forward caste) Congress leader.
5.	Dontali (Nellore, dist.)	In a mob attack one person of a Golla backward caste was killed by Kammas. He was instrumental in organizing labourers.
6.	Chirala (Prakasam, dist.)	The killers of the Karamchendu case again murdered an elderly dalit woman, Alisamma, a principal witness in the Karamchendu case.

(Contd.)

Sl.No.	Place of Occurrence	Nature of the Incident
7.	Bandlapalli (Chittoor, dist)	Four Dalits were beaten and stabbed to death in an assult by a group of Reddy and other forward caste men in a dispute over half an acre of cultivable waste.
8.	Kodavatikallu (Khrishna, dist.)	A dalit farm-servant was killed by Kamma landlord for disobedience.
9.	Beernakallu (Nellore, dist.)	Dalit labourer killed by youth of Kamma landlord families for coming in the way of their harassment of women.
10.	Gokarajupalli (Khrishna, dist.)	Dalit labourer was killed by youth of kamma landlord families for his intervention while they harass women.
11.	Tandutur (Prakasam, dist.)	A dalit woman was raped and set on fire and killed by a TDFP goon of Kamma caste.
12.	Jabbargudem (Rangareddy, dist.)	A dalit was killed in a mass assault at the behest of a Reddy landlord because Dalits of this area have organized and fought for land and wages.
13.	Pippara (West Godavari, dist.)	Dalit killed in a mass assault by Rajus castes (forward caste) directed by a local congress leader. Dalits had protested against molestation of dalit women by the youth of the Raju caste.
14.	Chinakada (Vizianagaram, dist.)	Four tribals, a father and three sons, killed in mass attack by Savarna Hindus at the behest of a liquor contractor, for illicitly brewing and selling liquor.
15.	Mandadam (Guntur, dist.)	Two Erukala tribals abducted, tortured and killed by man of fishing contractor for catching and selling fish on the sly.
16.	Pulivendula (Cuddapah, dist.)	More than 150 houses of Erukala tribes people set on fire and detonated by mob of Servarnas led by village Sarpanch and Congress (I) leader, Y.S. Raja Reddy, father of prominent Congressman Y.S. Rajasekhar Reddy.
17.	Nakkalampeta (Krishna, dist.)	Dalit farm servant was murdered by youth of landlord's household on suspicion of intimacy with woman of the house.
18.	Jeerupalem	About 180 houses of fishing community set on fire

(Contd.)

Sl.No.	*Place of Occurrence*	*Nature of the Incident*
	(Srikakulam, dist.)	by mob organized by prominent Congress (I) B C leader, big landlord, former minister and former Chairman, Zilla Parishad by name Gorle Sriramulu Naidu. The fishing people were fighting for return of 70 acres of their land grabbed by him.
19.	Gutlapadu (West Godavari, dist.)	Two Dalits were killed in a mass assault by men of Kapu caste (forward caste) numbering 2000 for questioning their dominance.
20.	Reddypalli (Rangareddy, dist.)	Erukala peasant burnt to death on pretext of sorcery by Reddy landlord close to local MLA for questioning the latter's dishonesty in a land deal.
21.	Kothapulavand-lapalli (Anantapur, dist.)	A Dalit was burnt alive by a mob of Reddy and other caste for his rebellious attitude.
22.	Vetlapalem (East Godavari, dist.)	Nearly hundred houses of Dalits set on fire and destroyed by Kamma landlords-cum-mill owners.
23.	Kaspa Gada-bavalasa (Vizianagaram, dist.)	Four tribals and a harijan killed by a mob of caste Hindus in connection with a land dispute involving 18 acres of land.
24.	Chillakallu (Krishna, dist.)	A dalit Sub-Inspector of Police shot himself dead as he could not bear the casteist harassment of the Kapu caste (forward caste) Circle-Inspector, his immediate superior.
25.	Moodurllpalli (Kurnool, dist.)	Dalit labourer beaten to death by Reddys for protesting against harassment of his wife by a Reddy.
26.	Ambaripet (Adilabad, dist.)	A Boya caste (backward caste) farm-servant shot dead by his landlord, G. Narahan Reddy, congress (I) leader, former MP, former Zilla Paishad Chairman and big landholder.
27.	Chundur (Guntur dist.)	17 dalits were massacred by a large mob of Reddy and some Kapu menin a savage attack as finale to a month-long period of conflict. An argument between a dalit youth and upper castes in a cinema Hall led to this massacre.

The above incidents make it amply clear that in post-independent India, Dalits had to pay a heavy price for asserting and demanding their civil, democratic and constitutional rights. Most of the above incidents clearly revealed that in post-independent India, Dalits have had to pay a heavy price for asserting their civil and constitutional rights. Most of the caste Hindu atrocities on dalits centred around the right of access to public wells, tanks, educational institutions, social dignity and equality (marriage processions along the streets, wearing clean clothes, chappals, etc.). Caste violence was also related to agrarian relations, i.e., access to grazing land, grants of government wastelands, demand for an increase in wages, etc. The life of Dalits was thought to be valueless and hence they were put to death on the mere suspicion of a theft. The Dalits accused were not even allowed to prove their innocence or exercise their legal/constitutional rights. The dominant upper castes brazenly took the law into their own hands and meted out punishments to Dalits. The extra-legal and constitutional authority and socio-economic power of the upper caste was demonstrated in order to force the Dalits to accept and respect their dominance in the villages. During 1990s the press and various enquiries/surveys in Andhra Pradesh revealed that the evil of untouchability continued to be extensively practiced and Dalits were defenseless against atrocities committed on them since police and revenue officials tended to support upper castes. On the floor of the state Assembly Legislative members mentioned numerous instances of caste discrimination against dalit such as abuse, harassment, molestation of women, disconnection of power supply to dalit colonies for protesting against discrimination and social boycott. It was also mentioned that there was no dearth of instances of temple entry to Dalits. The practice of preventing Dalits from drinking water from public taps, wearing footwear before upper castes and surrendering their seats in buses was prevalent throughout the state. "Even at a tea-stall near the MLA's hostel in Hyderabad, the weaker sections were forced to drink tea outside."[18]

NOTES AND REFERENCES

1. It is a part of my on-going research project on the social history of lower castes in Andhra Pradesh during the nineteenth and twentieth centuries. I have been consulting many vernacular sources pertaining to dalit literature and movements. My recent book, *Dalit and Upper*

Castes: Essays in Social History, Delhi, 2005, explored some important aspects of Dalit movement in modern Andhra.

2. Chinna Rao Yagati, *Dalits' Struggle for Identity: Andhra and Hyderabad, 1900-1950*, (New Delhi, 2003); V. Ramakrishna, *Social Reform in Andhra*, (New Delhi, 1983).
3. The speeches and essays are found in Bhagya Reddi Papers and biographical works of M.B. Gautham "The Untouchable Movement in Andhra Pradesh", in *Andhra Pradesh State Harijan Conference Souvenir*, Hyderabad, 10-12 April 1976; P.R. Venkata Swamy, *Our Struggle for Emancipation*, 2 vols., (Secunderabad, 1955).
4. Gail Omvedt, *Dalits and the Democratic Revolution in India*, (Delhi, 1994), p. 124.
5. A. Satyanarayana, *Dalits and Upper Castes, op. cit.*, pp. 86, 90.
6. Chinna Rao Yagati, *Dalits' Struggle for Identity, op. cit.*
7. A. Satyanarayana, *Dalits and Upper Castes, op. cit.*, p. 101.
8. *Ibid.*, pp. 87-88.
9. Gogu Shyamala, *Nalla Poddu*, (Hyderabad, 2003).
10. Chinna Rao Yagati, *Dalits' Struggle for Identity, op. cit.*, Chapter 5.
11. A. Satyanarayana, *Dalits and Upper Castes, op. cit.*, p. 88.
12. Chinna Rao Yagati, "Rise and Growth of Dalit Movement in Andhra", *Indian Social Science Review*, vol. 5, No.1, (2003).
13. For details see N.D. Kamble, *Atrocities on Scheduled Castes*, New Delhi, 1980.
14. This information is collected from a dalit weekly *Navajeevana*, October 26, 1947 and July 30, 1950; N.D. Kamble, *Atrocities on Scheduled Caste, op. cit.*
15. K.Prasad, *Dalit Movement in Andhra Pradesh* (Telugu), Vijayawada, 1994.
16. Ramnarayan S.Rawat, "The Problem" in *Seminar 558*, February 2006, p. 14.
17. See, *Economic and Political Weekly*, 19 October 1991, p. 2404.
18. *The Hindu*, 23 March 1999.

4

Complexities of the Dalit Movement in India

RAJ SEKHAR BASU

Over a hundred years or more, Dalits have waged a long struggle for emancipation from the oppressive caste discrimination and the inhuman practice of untouchability. They have also been vocal against economic exploitation and the marginalized political participation of the erstwhile untouchable communities in both colonial and post colonial India.[1] In the recent past the publication of the Mandal Commission report and the subsequent adoption of its recommendations by both the central and the provincial governments of India not only led to a caste Hindu backlash but also raised serious questions about the implications of caste consciousness in secular India.[2] Prior to and soon after independence, there had been major debates as to whether the caste system was conducive or inimical to modernization, economic development, industrialization and democracy. As early as 1921, Max Weber had pointed out that caste system and the Hindu social order would be major impediments to the development of capitalism.[3] After independence, a few scholars had taken the same position.[4] But, a few others have emphasized on the flexible and adoptive nature of the caste system.[5] Interestingly, within a decade following the Indian independence, Selig Harrison had opined that caste served as a basis for economic and political competition and in the process magnified its worst features. Thus, there was a presumption that caste in the absence of well-articulated interest groups would function as a sort of an improvised infrastructure for democracy.[6] Significantly, the early 1990s happened to be one of the most troubled periods in India's post-colonial history. In fact, caste came to be recognized as a major mobilizing factor. There was also a belief that caste could provide the basis for a platform against communalism and hierarchical order in contemporary Indian society.[7] But the restiveness on the part of the upper castes over the issue of reservation raised serious apprehensions about the divisive impact of articulated caste consciousness in India. The growing incidents of violence, involving the Dalit communities and the upper castes convinced some of the enlightened groups in the Indian society that assertion of caste identity could lead to a destabilization of the political sovereignty of the "nation state".[8] Presumably, it is in the light of these developments that an academic exercise needs to be undertaken over the question of caste identity and that of its role in nation building. Such an exercise assumes importance because since the last phase of colonial rule the nationalists had attempted to reconcile caste identity with the other features of Indian pluralism, ostensibly to lay the foundations of a strong anti-imperialist mass movement. Thus, it becomes imperative to unearth the history of identity formation in the colonial period and the politics of protest associated with it.

In the past several decades, scholars dealing with 'untouchable' communities have focused on a wide range of issues. In the first place, there had been an inclination to understand the reasons behind the origin and development of agrestic servitude in different parts of India. Scholars involved with such studies were more interested in unearthing the specificities of the historical context in which the system of bondage emerged and developed some of its distinctive features. Secondly, in some other studies, scholars placed a greater deal of emphasis in understanding the factors responsible for the formation of distinct lower caste identities, which were sometimes opposed to that of the 'nation'. These studies placed a great deal of emphasis on the growth of lower caste consciousness, role of caste associations and the political strategies pursued by the lower caste politicians in the wake of the institutional concessions offered by the colonial government as well as by the governments of the native states. Thirdly, there have been studies, which have emphasized on the ramifications of Dalit consciousness in contemporary times. It has been argued that the usage of terms such as 'national community' and 'national culture' reflects the story of upper caste domination over different subaltern social groups within the nation. Lastly, there have been some studies, which have tried to understand the contemporary social behaviour of the 'untouchable' communities. Scholars engaged in such studies have tried to explore the attitudes of the 'untouchable' communities towards the prevailing caste system.

The narrative on agrarian bondage should essentially begin with the opinions expressed by Dharma Kumar in this regard. In her research, Dharma Kumar had argued that the bonded labourers belonged to the lowest of the Hindu 'castes' and were in many places just 'untouchables' having no recognized position in the caste system. She argued that caste not only confirmed the social and economic disadvantages of the agricultural labourer, but also gave him some rights, some of which were economic, while others were of a social and ritual nature. The most important of these rights was that of working on a piece of land. The landholder had the obligation to employ him on the land and pay him the customary wages. In this sense, it was argued that the labourers were not landless.[9] However this right had no substance whatsoever. The land which the labourer tilled was not his own and he essentially remained a labourer. About the so-called 'customary wages' Dharma Kumar herself qualifies her statement: 'although the serf may have had some right to a share in the produce of his land, he had fewer economic rights than the mirasidar or tenant; his share of the produce was very much smaller'.[10] This is a gross under statement on deprivations suffered by the bonded labourers.

Benedicte Hjejle on the basis of the early colonial documents noted an invariable association of 'agricultural bondage' with the mirasi form of land tenure, and also the concentration of bondage in the wet farming areas, particularly in the rice farming regions.[11] While the rise of the mirasi right had much to do with wet farming, the records did not clearly explain the causal relationship of mirasi right and bondage. However, two conclusions emerge from the records. In the first place, caste system did not create bondage. Secondly, once the mirasidars became involved in new agricultural settlements, they came to acquire a nearly exclusive monopoly over the village land and the labourers, on whom they could depend, partly because of cultural and partly of economic reasons. Mirasi literally meaning inheritance, was a privileged tenure, the privileges amounting to ownership in the lands brought under cultivation by the mirasidars.[12] Incidentally the communal nature of the agricultural organization also led to a communal control over the bonded labour, the major labour force in agriculture. It was this communal nature of mirasi control over bonded labour that distinguished it from what Hjejle called 'a more personal kind of slavery', which resulted when labourers sold 'themselves or their relations to individual farmers'.[13]

Benedicte Hjejle also argued that the anti-slavery legislations of the early 1840s did not bring about a great change in the conditions of the bonded labourers, belonging mostly to the 'untouchable' communities in Tamilnadu. In fact, the legislation was brought to the notice of the Indian officials, who almost exclusively belonged to the higher castes and many of whom were slave owners themselves. As a result, it gave them an opportunity to think of methods by which they could keep their slaves or serfs in obedience.[14] But, it was argued that emigration did provide opportunities to some of the returned emigrees to become independent farmers. Hjejle argued that this success was directly correlated to the weakening of the mirasi system in districts like Trichinopoly and South Arcot, where waste land was available on reasonable terms and the Paraiyans returning from abroad could utilise their savings to establish themselves as small cultivators.[15]

Baker's authoritative study on the rural economy of Tamilnadu assumed the existence of a sharply polarised society, both in material as well as ritual terms. But he did not adequately explain the origins of this bipolarity; particularly the process through which a distinctive bonded labour came to form the basis of the village agricultural organization. In the context of the bipolarized village society in the valley region (the two other distinct regions being the plains and Kongunad), Baker emphasized that the economic foundation was laid around the development of irrigated rice agriculture. It was also argued that the Vellalas ('lord of the land') were mostly migrants from the west coast and were initially the people who had 'landed wealth' and 'good stock'. The source of their landed status and power associated with it was presumably their enterprise in the organization of the wet farming. The 'ritual division' between this group and the hoi polloi of slaves and servants largely resulted from the conscious efforts of the Vellalas to mark them off culturally from the rest.[16] At the same time, it has been suggested that the persons who formed the bonded labour force for the cultivation of land nearly monopolized by the Vellala – Brahmin combination, were migrants from the 'plains' region.

David Ludden suggests a more fruitful line of investigation into the origins of this labour force. He observed, 'Pandya wars with tribal chiefs probably procured workers from the defeated populations, because both major landless laborer castes–Pallas and Pariahs – boast even today distant martial traditions....'[17] He also cites an oral tradition in which the Pallas were called 'mountain people' who settled in the plains. 'This change of milieu might have been forced on them by wars with Pandya armies, although, on the other hand, primitive cultivators from the hills or plains might have voluntarily exchanged their precarious independence for better-fed subservient status in irrigated villages.'[18] It has been argued that the power that enabled the landowners to exclude the 'immigrants' from control over land and also to dispossess the 'local residents' off the land they had been controlling had presumably nothing to do with the so-called caste sanctions.

Arun Bandopadhyay has argued that in those areas of Tamilnadu, where the big mirasidars had a virtual monopoly in land ownership, the lands were cultivated either through *pallans,* the bonded labourers, or through *parakudis,* their under-tenants. The cultivation of land was carried out in three different systems. The first system was called "*pannai*" system in both Tanjore and Trichinopoly, under which the mirasidars cultivated their lands with the assistance of Pannaiyals or farm labourers who were paid daily wages. The second method of cultivation was known as *varam* or sharing system. The mirasidar and the *parakudis* (generally non-resident cultivators) under this system were jointly concerned with the cultivation of the land. The share of the *parakudi* was called *parakudi varam*. The third system of cultivation was the lease system. This method was adopted by the non-resident mirasidars, who shared none of the risks of cultivation and got only a stipulated quantity of grain out of total produce of their lands.[19]

Though the pannaiyal system of cultivation was the most profitable to the mirasidars, the *varam* system was more common.

The domination of the big mirasidars was the most marked feature in Tanjore. Mostly the slaves and servants of the mirasidars carried on the cultivation. In Tinnevelli, the mirasidars had a controlling power over the labour of the *parakudis* and pannaiyals. This sort of control was evident from two systems. The first was the system of *kudimaramat,* for repair of river channels, tanks etc., and was based on customary labour and, in some places on bonded labour. The second system of exploiting labour services was the compulsory work on roads. The Paraiyans and Pallans were mostly compelled to do such work. In the wet taluks of Trichinopoly, the mirasidars had a similar control over land and labour.[20] Bandopadhyay has argued that one significant feature of the various forms of labour in Tamil agriculture was a certain degree of mobility, particularly amongst groups which included small peasant-owners, tenants, hired labour and even occasionally bonded labour. The small peasant was particularly quick in moving from one area to other, or in changing the very form of his labour, as the situation demanded. But as far as the tenants were concerned, the increasing trend was to demand the ownership status through pattas, particularly in areas where mirasi right was not strong and land was becoming waste. In the 1840s a few bonded labourers in Trichinopoly wanted to own land left waste by the mirasidars.[21] Finally, there were significant changes in the strength of the mirasi right vis-a-vis the forms of labour in the second quarter of the nineteenth century.[22]

In his brief study of the 'Pariah' (agricultural labour caste) in late eighteenth century South India, Washbrook has pointed to the non-existence of long term bondage of labourers. He observed, "...relations of personal, long-term servitude... were common only in limited parts of the Kaveri delta (and in Malabar on the West Coast). Outside the most intensive zones of 'wet' agriculture (that is over the great mass of South India) they were scarcely found...no class of *adimai* (except perhaps on the West Coast) was without personal rights or treatable as simple chattel slaves".[23] The wider economic system of the late eighteenth century was characterized by labour scarcity and a fair degree of diversification resulting largely from the recurring wars. The issue of labour scarcity has not been adequately explained, nor has its magnitude been quantified. It has been argued that the personal right of the 'Pariahs' was widely recognized. There was also a belief that the existence of a highly developed pastoralist sector of the economy 'made the 'Pariahs' very much property owning in other regards, such as livestock'. Such conditions, though conducive to the mobility of labour, did not however preclude arrangements, formal or otherwise, for long-term ties with their masters. Labour scarcity and unstable political and economic conditions prompted the masters to keep the labourers tied for long periods. However, the masters, means of preventing desertions of labourers were rather limited and few.

Haruka Yanagisawa in his research has focused on the changes in land ownership since the mid-nineteenth century. He pointed to the decline of upper caste dominance in land holding and the increase in landownership by the newly rich belonging to the Chettiyar and other trading communities.[24] The new owners lacking experience in the sphere of labour management, favoured short term tenancy (or occasionally share cropping) as a source of stable rental income. The utilization of bonded labour was reduced to the extent that short-term tenancy was substituted for long-term bondage as a mode of land management.[25] It has also been argued that emigration and internal migration of bonded labour in the last decades of the nineteenth century affected the system of bondage.[26]

Gunnel Cederlof's study of bondage in the Coimbatore district in the Kongunad region of Tamilnadu points to the impact of industrial and economic development on the labour force, which had already been depleted by emigration at the turn of the twentieth century. She has argued that there was a direct correlation between 'development' and 'bondage'.[27] It has been pointed out that in the early nineteenth century, the agriculturists in the high lands did not have to depend on labourers like their counterparts in the wet cultivation areas. However, scarcity of labour developed in the years between 1900 and 1930 and this actually tended to strengthen the bondage of the Madhari labourers in the region.[28]

More recently, B.B. Chaudhuri has argued that the undue emphasis on the role of caste in the demand for bonded labour and its supply as well needs to be corrected. He states that caste only partly explains the demand. Its role in the supply is also doubtful. At the same time, it is also not clear as to how caste by itself created a landless group. In all probability, the group somehow lost land and later came to be placed at the lowest rung of the caste hierarchy or kept outside the caste organization. Thus, the landless people with few opportunities of finding employment elsewhere were easily drawn into the agricultural organization dominated by the landowners. Subsequently, the degraded social position of the labourers and their nearly complete separation from the wider society, where they were regarded as 'untouchables', tended to sap any will to rise in the estimation of society and to break away from their bondage. Even where they had the will, it has been argued, they failed to unite, because of their division into several sub castes.[29]

In the case of Kerala, K. Saradamoni argued that the dependence of the Pulaya agricultural labourers on the Brahmin landowners for their living forced them to accept a state of bondage. At the same time, the laws and customs of the upper castes led to a proliferation of the categories of 'untouchables' and 'slaves' in the society. In the case of the Pulayas, the landlords enforced their control by emphasizing on purity and pollution. The government initially was reluctant in abolishing slavery, since it believed that it would harm its own interests and destroy the sanctity of private property.[30] The government also felt that compared to the system of slavery prevalent in the West Indies, slavery in Kerala was mild in its features and did not elicit any drastic legal action.

In his research dealing with the Kamias of South Bihar, Gyan Prakash has argued that bondage was a legal construct, 'a creation of British legal concepts'. The new juridical representation reduced bondage to 'debt bondage'. The juridical representation of debt bondage reduced Kamias to bonded labourers.[31] Prakash was also in favour of excluding the 'outcastes' and servile dependents from the category of agricultural labourers. He objects to their inclusion on the ground that 'their identification as labourers meant stripping the social and the ideological, (outcaste, servile) from the economic (labour).'[32]

Gyan Prakash has related bondage to two features of the region's agricultural organization: one of a general nature, 'agricultural seasonality' and the other more specific, 'the predominance of paddy cultivation'. But, it was monocropping of rice, which made the difference. The demand for labour sharply fell in the south in the post-harvest weeks. Unlike in the north where 'double-cropping was widely practiced', the labourers in the south had nothing to fall back upon. This sort of situation favoured the creation of special bonds between the labourers and the landowners.[33]

In the case of South Gujarat, Jan Breman has admitted that the caste ban on the direct involvement of the Brahmins in agriculture necessitated dependence on labour. In fact, bonded labour system (halipratha) was particularly noticeable in regions with an intensive crop system, especially where the labour-intensive cultivation of sugarcane was considerable. The motive of the landlords in keeping bonded labourers was guided by their interests to ensure the required labour supply at the peaks of agrarian cycle, when the normally abundant supply of labour turned into severe shortage.[34] Breman attributed the decline of the hali system partly to the falling demand for hali labour,due to the shrinking of sugar acreage, sugarcane cultivation being the most labour intensive. In this case, Breman admitted the expanding market system undermined much of the old relationship that had developed when the market was limited.[35]

Incidentally, scholars interested in the history of the lower caste movements have been drawn less towards the debates relating to agrestic servitude. In fact, they have focussed more on weaknesses of the nationalist movement. The nationalist movement has been to a large extent interpreted as a Hindu high caste affair.[36] It has been stated that Gandhi's involvement did not bring about a radical change. Sekhar Bandopadhyay has argued that the earlier nationalist historiography, with an *a priori* assumption of an ideological hegemony of nationalism, almost completely ignored this phenomenon.[37] He has stated that some of the recent historians have tried to explain it in terms of failure of mobilisation or as a manifestation of subaltern passivity.[38]

More recently, scholars have emphasised on the necessity of exploring the mentality of the marginal groups, like those of the lower caste Hindus and the Muslims, who in the nineteenth century were believed to have developed their own social identities, which were sometimes opposed to that of the 'nation'.[39] Their construction of a new collective self-identity reflected their own perceptions of power relations prevailing within the colonial society and of their own location within it. Presumably, such initiatives led them to define colonial rule in their own terms, which in most cases differed substantially from that of mainstream nationalism. In a sense, the well-defined lower caste identities contradicted the nationalist ideology that was expoused by the upper caste Hindus. Yet, as Sekhar Bandopadhyay has pointed out over emphasis on these identities 'trivialises both fissions within the former and overlapping of the two'.[40]

Significantly, there have been several other scholarly interpretations of the lower caste movements. In the 1960s and 1970s, it was often opined that these movements resulted from the economic and social ambitions of some upwardly mobile communities. The elite leaders of these communities were believed to have organised these movements for gaining a higher ritual status that was commensurate to their newly improved secular status. These leaders followed Sanskritic norms and rituals and also invented their own caste mythologies to achieve such goals. The movements of the Nadars and Ezhavas of south India are possibly the best examples of such a trend. The Nadars of Tamilnadu organised themselves in the late nineteenth century to free themselves from the social disabilities from which they suffered. Robert Hardgrave (Jr.) has pointed out that such efforts led to the social as well as political uplift of the Nadars. In other words, the Nadars moved up from the lower rungs of the ritual hierarchy to a position of status and power. Hardgrave has argued that this change was brought about by the Nadar Mahajan Sangam, which claimed to represent the community as a whole.[41]

The Ezhavas also formed their own caste association in 1903. The Sri Narayana Dharma Paripalana Yogam (hereafter SNDP Yogam) serving as the caste association laid emphasis on the sanskritisation of the norms and rituals of the Ezhavas. In the 1920s, the Ezhavas participated in temple entry satyagrahas and negotiated with the government for gaining more economic and political privileges.[42] In Western India, the adoption of new occupations as well as the economic mobility forced the Mahar community leaders to launch bigger movements for self-respect and equality.[43] Incidentally, in the researches dealing with the lower caste movements in southern and western India, there had been an inclination to establish the point that the elite leadership initially had attempted to acquire symbols of high status. The leaders were believed to have focussed on the material sources of high status i.e. education, employment and political power.

But there are certain problems with such interpretations. In fact, such studies wholly ignored the elements of protest that were inherent in all such movements. In the case of the Namasudras of Eastern Bengal, Sekhar Bandopadhyay has argued that despite appropriating certain symbols of authority, the lower caste leaders strongly protested against the inequitous distribution of political and economic opportunities.[44] But there are some other scholars who only see deprivation and protest in such movements. They argue that built-up resentments against an unequal social order gave rise to these movements. Such ideas were expressed by K. Saradamoni in her researches on the Pulayas of Kerala. She argued that the Pulaya leader Ayyankali influenced by Ezhava reformers organised protest movements in search of social freedom.[45] Swaraj Basu in his research has pointed out that the Rajbansis constituted the largest caste group in Bengal. Their origin remained mired in mystery and there was a debate over their associations with the Kochs. But, whatever may have been their origin; there is little doubt that they were the early settlers in North Bengal. However, the migration of the upper caster gentry into the traditional Rajbansi bastions led to significant changes in the economy of the region. The immigrants not only gained control over the land but also were also successful in establishing their dominance over the local administration. Consequently, the Rajbansis were turned into sharecroppers in the lands, which they once owned. The change in the socio-economic status of Rajbansis prompted a section of them to claim an equality of status with the upper castes. But, their failures in this regard led them to forge a new identity. In fact, it was from a sense of socio-economic deprivation as well as out of attempts to achieve a higher social status that the Rajbansi movement originated.[46]

Vijay Prashad has argued that the inadequate nature of the programmes offered by the Hindu reformers led to the growth of radical sentiments among the Dalit communities of Punjab. The spokesmen of the radical Dalits, who had already been drawn towards the Adi-Dharm movement, expressed their resentment towards Brahmanical customs and values. They asserted the glorious aboriginal past of the Dalits, who had been the original settlers of this region. However, the Adi-Dharm movement failed to fulfil the expectations of the exploited Dalit communities. Apart from the apathetic attitude of the government and that of the militant Hindus, the fissures between the Chuhras and the Chamars eliminated all the hopes of a radical Dalit movement. Yet, there seemed to have been a resurgence of Balmiki identity. This identity largely emerged from the activities of Arya Samaj activist like Ami Chand, who worked under the banner of Dalitudhar Mandal.[47] In 1936, Ami Chand wrote the *Valmiki Prakash,* the staple tract of the Balmiki community. In this tract the Adi-Dharm leaders such as Achutananda and Shrudananda, were criticized, since they had sought to separate the Dalits from the Hindus.[48] It was strongly stated that Adi Hindus were not a religious community and that Kabirdas and Raidas had been worshippers of Ram and Krishna. Valmiki was chosen as the guru, because gurus were necessary to overcome the difficulties in human life. Such thoughts were aptly summarized in the statement, "Guru bin gati nehin, Shah bin pati nehin".[49]

However, the efforts of the Blamikis to find a place within the Hindu fold did not deter them to respond to the radical language of class that had surfaced during the last days of the nationalist struggle. As in the case of the Namasudras and the Rajbansis, the Balmikis too were drawn towards the Communist Party of India. The communist involvement with the sweeper's strike under the banner of the Safai Majdur Sangh forced the Congress to arrange for state packages to the Balmikis. By the late 1950s, the Balmikis themselves had become divided along the lines of ideologies. While some were drawn to the Congress, others were attracted towards Hindutva. There was another section which favoured the preservation of the primordial cultural values that were an integral part of Dalitism. Nonetheless, the presence of the Communist Parties in the Dalit localities of Delhi kept alive the hopes of a struggle.[50]

Chinna Rao Yagati has pointed out that in the first half of the twentieth century in the Telugu speaking regions of the Madras Presidency, the Dalits organized themselves under the flag of the Adi Andhra Movement. This movement as a precursor to the Gandhian programme of Harijan uplift sought to articulate the grievances of the Dalit communities through a radical emancipatory ideology—that was opposed to the nationalist discourse. In the 1930s, the appropriation of the Dalits into the Congress fold through the activities of the Harijan Sevak Sangh accounted for the debacle of the Adi Andhra movement in coastal Andhra. The communist led agrarian movements also posed a challenge to the radical Dalit leadership. Incidentally, both the Congress and the Communist opposition created anti Ambedkar feelings and encouraged factionalism in Dalit politics. In such a situation, the caste Hindu leadership of the different political parties were able to integrate the Dalits to their own distinct brand of politics.[51]

Sourabh Dube's research has also emphasised on the elements of protest among the Satnamis against the established traditions of the Hindu social order. It has been pointed out that throughout the nineteenth and twentieth centuries, the perceptions of the Satnamis vis-a-vis the Hindu social order, fashioned a distinct identity—amalgamating the features of a caste and a sect. The articulation of this identity found expression in the petitions sent to the provincial government by the Satnami Mahasabha in the 1920s.[52]

Sociologists like Surinder Singh Jodhka have argued that the Adi-Dharm movement started by Manguram from the very beginning saw itself as a new religious movement. The Adi-Dharmis asserted that the 'untouchables' did constitute a separate *quam*, i.e. a distinct religious community on the lines of the Hindus, Muslims and Sikhs.[53] Mark Juergensmeyer in his research on the Adi-Dharmis has also asserted that the Adi-Dharmis insisted on being labelled as a separate religious grouping and did not favour any attempt to club them with the Hindus.[54] The demand of the Adi-Dharmis to be enlisted as a separate faith met with stiff opposition from the upper caste Hindus. But, later this demand was accepted. In fact, the majority of the lower castes of Jalandhar and Hoshiarpur enlisted themselves as Adi-Dharmis during the enumeration drives undertaken for the 1931 Punjab census.[55] Subsequently, the Adi-Dharm movement was appropriated by Dr. B.R.Ambedkar's All India Scheduled Caste Federation. Though Ambedkar gained a great deal of popularity among the Adi-Dharmis, but only a few of them supported his call for conversion to Buddhism.[56]

Christophe Jaffrelot has stated that the Chamar leader, Swami Achhutanand in his Adi Hindu philosophy had put forth the view that the 'untouchables' were the first inhabitants of India, the rightful owners of the land. The Aryans were alleged to have destroyed their culture and civilization and made them 'untouchables' in the society. Swami Achutanand popularised the view that the Adi Hindus had their roots in the Indus Valley Civilization of Harappa and Mohenjo Daro.[57] Significantly, there have been other interpretations of the lower caste movements. Ghanshyam Shah has classified these movements in two broad categories–reformative and alternative.

The former advocated the reform of the caste system to solve the problem of untouchability.[58] On the other hand, the alternative movements attempted to create an alternative socio-cultural structure by encouraging conversion to some other religion or by laying emphasis on education, economic status and political power. The anti-untouchability movement launched by B.R. Ambedkar in the early decades of the twentieth century in Maharastra had all the features of an alternative movement. The movement spread to different parts of the country and came to acquire an all India character. Ambedkar strongly stressed that the 'untouchables' needed to acquire political power to achieve social and economic equality with the highest classes in the modern society.[59]

Gail Omvedt has interpreted the lower caste movements as 'anti-systematic movements', seeking to transform the basic structure of the Indian social system. It has been argued that these movements sought to replace caste and other types of social and political oppression through the establishment of an egalitarian society. Such movements were believed to have been akin to radical Marxism, as they attempted to destroy the branches of an old feudalistic social order.[60] Partha Chatterjee has argued that though the lower caste movements often inspired by popular cults and sects deviated from the dominant Hindu Dharma, nevertheless they selectively appropriated the ideological resources of accepted cultural traditions and also transformed them to cope with the conditions of subordination. In a sense, these movements attempted to turn the constituted order upside down.[61] It has also been argued that despite their opposition to mainstream nationalism, these movements were not anti-nationalist. As M.S.S. Pandian has pointed out, that the lower castes looked for a nation based on the principle of substantive, instead of the nominal citizenship that was being offered by the Congress.[62]

It has also been pointed out that the nationalist invocation of Vedic civilization led to the hierarchisation of different social groups, who were finally accomodated within the nation. But, the dominant nationalism accomodated them only as inferiors within the nation. Thus, to carve out a space for those outside the pale of civilization, articulate sections of the Dalits (a term used for the erstwhile 'untouchable' communities) supported cultural practices, which were looked upon as 'lowly' by the upper caste Hindus. Beef-eating, drinking and speaking in Dalit dialect became important features of this cultural politics.[63]

In the past two decades, some anthropologists and sociologists undertook studies of different communities to explore the cultural interactions between the Dalits (a term now being used for erstwhile untouchable communities) and the upper caste Hindus. In most cases, these studies examined Louis Dumont's hypothesis regarding hierarchy. Michael Moffat's study of an 'untouchable' community in Tamilnadu may be taken as valid example of such a trend. Moffat argued that there were relatively few cultural discontinuities between the 'untouchable' and the higher castes in the village of Endavur. The 'untouchables' formed part of a 'Harijan sub system', in which the low castes were ranked and ordered in very much the same way as the other castes. This rank order, as in the caste system was kept in place by exclusivity in marriage, commensal inclusion and exclusion based on the notions of purity and pollution. Thus, it was claimed that the 'untouchables' agreed with their caste co-villagers in far more respects than they disagreed with them.[64]

Robert Deliege on the basis of fieldwork in the village of Valghira Manickam, situated in the Ramnathaparam district of Tamilnadu, argued that though the 'untouchables' have upheld 'untouchability' with regard to other inferior castes, this should not lead us to a conclusion that they have accepted their own degraded status. The 'Paraiyars' have shown little inclination to incorporate Hindu ideas in their religious beliefs. The 'Paraiyars' have often violenthy opposed the attempts on the part of the dominant social groups to impose humiliations upon them on the pretext that they were 'untouchables', living on the frontiers of the Hindu society.[65]

David Mosse, in one of his articles has argued that Pallars (a 'untouchable' community in Tamilnadu) employed new identities to maximise their access to material and political resources and to promote their interests and caste standing.[66] He also argues that religion and purity are not separable from politics and power from the point of view of Harijan subordination and dependence. This position, according to Mosse, eliminates all possibilities of an autonomous subaltern culture.

In the case of northern India, anthropologists and sociologists have expressed different views about the social behaviour of the 'untouchable' communities. Gerald Berreman in his researches based on the villages of the Himalayan region had argued that though the low caste people resented the polluted status ascribed to them, they had few opportunities to express this resentment due to the economic power held by the high castes.[67] In the case of Agra, Owen Lynch has pointed out that the Jatavs, like many other castes tried to sanskritize their practices that are to adopt the ritual practices of the higher castes to achieve status.[68] Such attempts were seldom successful and the Jatavs later converted to Buddhism to secure respectability. Margaret Searle-Chatterjee has argued that 'untouchable' communities seldom used the word 'Hindu', while referring to themselves. This could be interpreted as a conscious and principled rejection of the caste system or simply as lack of identification with 'others' who called themselves Hindus.[69]

Incidentally, the considerations of the electoral market have led to 'vigorous marketing' of caste mobilization strategies in favour of the various political forces which are active in democratic electoral politics. In the wake of the Mandal Commission report, the lower castes and Dalit groups in several parts of India became politically assertive. As Badri Narayan has argued these groups became aware that power was embedded in their caste vote bank and in their efforts to mobilize a combined Bahujan Dalit identity.[70] In other words, this encouraged the lower caste groups such as the Pasis to acquire a double identity – 'as members of a specific caste reiterating their caste pride and also as an important Dalit-Bahujan community that made sacrifices for the nation'[71] It has been argued that this double identity of the Dalit castes did encourage the writing of a new history, which was different if not opposed to the sanskritic model of caste history writing of the colonial period. These caste histories in the form of Gourav Gathas glorified Dalit socio cultural positions and instilled an element of self-respect among these castes. Yet, some of the remnants of the sanskritising features of these caste histories have enabled the Hindutva forces to appropriate the lower caste origin myths for their own political advantages. The Hindutva forces have been reinterpreting Dalit myths histories as well as symbols to project the Dalits as the defenders of Hindu dharma and as groups advocating the logic of nationalism.[72]

Finally, a question may be raised as to what are the real implications of Dalit movement and Dalit identity in contemporary India. In fact, the contemporary Dalit movement seems to have developed a large literature that has been able to create, strengthen as well as sustain a Dalit identity.[73] As Shalini Ramachandran has observed, such writings convey a pervasive sense of anger prevalent among the Dalits, who have by now realized 'that their failures were neither necessary nor inevitable'[74] Nonetheless, even when the Dalits are building up resistance against upper caste oppression, internal divisions, caste sentiments and caste ideology continue to impede their radical plans of protest. It has sometimes been argued that differential access to power and position has fuelled such a trend. But, the fact remains that Dalits continue to remain divided and they also continue to practice social discriminations against communities, which could also be lebelled as Dalits. This has led to a new system of hierarchy, which has a definite resemblance to the model of caste hierarchy, as practiced over a large part of the country.[75]

NOTES AND REFERENCES

1. V. Suresh, "The Dalit Movement in India" in T.V. Sathyamurthy (ed.), *Region, Religion, Caste, Gender and Culture in Contemporary India,* Oxford University Press, Delhi, 1996, p. 355; also see, Chinna Rao Yagati, *Dalits' Struggle for Identity: Andhra and Hyderabad 1900-1950,* Kanishka Publishers, Distributors, New Delhi, 2003, p. 1.
2. Sekhar Bandopadhyay, *Caste, Protest and Identity in Colonial India: The Namasudras of Bengal, 1872-1947,* Curzon, Richmond, 1997, p. 1.
3. Max-Weber. *The Religion of India,* The Free Press, Illinois, 1958.
4. For more details see, G.K. Karanth, "Caste after fifty years of Independence", *Review of Development and Change.* July-December, 1997, Vol. II, No. 2, p. 320
5. For more details see, Milton Singer, *When a Great Tradition Modernizes,* Praeger Publishers, New York, Washington and London, 1972; also see, 'Introduction: The Modernization of Occupational Cultures in South Asia' in Milton Singer (ed.) *Entrepreneurship and Modernization of Occupational Cultures in South Asia,* Duke University, Program of Comparative Studies in Southern Asia, Monograph Number 12, 1973 pp. 1-15.
6. Selig Harrison, *India: The Most Dangerous Decades,* Princeton University Press, Princeton, New Jersey, 1960.

7. Sekhar Bandopadhyay, Caste, Protest and Indentity in Colonial India, *op. cit*, p. 1
8. For more details see, *Indian Express*, (New Delhi), October 25, 1996.
9. Dharma Kumar, *Land and Caste in South India: Agricultural Labour in the Madras Presidency During the Nineteenth Century*, Manohar (Reprinted with an Introduction), New Delhi, 1992, p. 34.
10. *Ibid.*
11. Benedicte Hjejle, " Slavery and Agricultural Bondage in South India in the Nineteenth Century", *The Scandinavian Economic History Review*, Vol. XV, Nos. 1-2, 1967.
12. *Ibid.*, p. 78.
13. *Ibid.*, p. 81.
14. *Ibid.*, p. 98.
15. *Ibid.*, p. 125.
16. Baker observed, "Those local residents and immigrants whom the elites managed to exclude from control of land were still attracted to live in the valleys where the fertility of the fields guaranteed a fairly secure food supply (the alternative was to risk an independent existence in the harsh climate of the plains). The Brahmans and Vellalas could thus delegate the work of cultivation to others while they themselves concentrated on more cultural pursuits. They also managed to emphasise the enormous social and cultural difference between those who controlled the land and those who worked it". For more details see, C.J. Baker *An Indian Rural Economy, 1880-1955 : The Tamilnad Countryside*, Oxford University Press, Delhi, 1984, p. 29.
17. David Ludden, *Peasant History in South India*, Oxford University Press, Delhi 1989, p. 91.
18. *Ibid.*
19. Arun Bandopadhyay, *The Agrarian Economy of Tamilnadu, 1820-1855*, K.P. Bagchi & Company, Calcutta, 1992. pp. 229-231.
20. Arun Bandopadhyay, The Agrarian Economy of Tamilnadu, *op. cit.*, pp. 232-233.
21. *Ibid*, pp. 99-100.
22. Bandopadhyay has cited a number of cases, where the landowners faced a stiff challenge from the parakudi undertenants. See *Ibid*. pp. 228-236.
23. David Washbrook, "Land and Labour in Late Eighteenth Century South India: The Golden Age of the Pariah?" in Peter Robb (ed) *Dalit*

Movements and the Meanings of Labour in India, Oxford University Press, Delhi, 1993. p. 70.

24. Haruka Yanagisawa, *A Century of Change: Caste and Irrigated Lands in Tamilnadu, 1860s-1970s,* Manohar, New Delhi, 1996, pp. 151-160.
25. Haruka Yanagisawa, A Century of Change, *op. cit.,* pp. 95-97.
26. *Ibid.,* pp. 60-64.
27. Gunnel Cederlof, *Bonds Lost: Subordination, Conflict and Mobilisation in Rural South India, C.1900-1970,* Manohar, New Delhi, 1997, Chapter 3, 'Development and Bondage'.
28. *Ibid.,* pp. 113-115.
29. B. B. Chaudhuri, "Reopening The Question of Bonded Labour in Colonial India" in *The Calcutta Historical Journal* Vol. XVIII, No. 2, July-December, 1996. pp. 98-99.
30. K. Saradamoni, *Emergence of a Slave Caste: Pulayas of Kerala,* People's Publishing House, New Delhi, 1989, pp. 67-68.
31. Gyan Prakash, *Bonded Histories: Genealogies of Labour Servitude in Colonial India,* Cambridge University Press, 1990. The study concentrated on the Kamias (bonded labourers) of South Bihar. p. 140 and p. 142.
32. Gyan Prakash (ed.) *The World of Rural Labourer in Colonial India,* Oxford University Press, Delhi, 1992, p. 14.
33. Gyan Prakash, *Bonded Histories, op. cit.,* p. 32.
34. Jan Breman, *Patronage and Exploitation: Changing Agrarian Relations in South Gujrat, India,* 1st Publication, 1974; Reprint by Manohar, New Delhi, 1979, pp. 42-43.
35. *Ibid,* p. 79.
36. See, V. Suresh, "The Dalit Movement in India" in T.V. Satyamurthy (ed.) *Region, Religion, Caste, Gender and Culture in Contemporary India,* Vol. III, Oxford University Press,Delhi 1998, pp. 361-362 ; Kancha Ilaiah, "Dalitism vs. Brahminism : The Epistemological Conflict in History" in Ghanshyam Shah (ed.) *Dalit Identity and Politics, Cultural Subordination and Dalit Challenge,* Vol. 2, Sage, New Delhi, 2001, pp. 124-126 ; Narender Kumar, "Dalit and Shudra Politics and Anti Brahmin Movement" *Economic and Political Weekly,* Vol. XXXV, No. 45, November 4-10, 2000, p. 3977.
37. Sekhar Bandopadhyay, Caste, Protest and Identity in Colonial India *op. cit.,* p. 2.
38. *Ibid.*
39. For more details See, Rosalind O'Hanlon, *Caste, conflict and ideology: Mahatma Jotirao Phule and Low Caste Protest in nineteenth century Western*

India, Cambridge University Press, Cambridge, 1985; Eleanor Zelliot, *From Untouchable to Dalit: Essays on the Ambedkar Movement*, Manohar, Delhi, 1996; Gail Omvedt, *Dalits and the Democratic revolution: Dr. B. R. Ambedkar and the Dalit Movement in colonial India*, Sage, New Delhi, Thousand Oaks, London, 1994; Dilip M. Menon, *Caste, nationalism and communism in south India : Malabar 1900-1948*, Cambridge University Press, New Delhi, 1994; Mohan Ram, 'Ramaswami Naickar and the Dravidian Movement', *Economic and Political Weekly*, Annual Number, February, 1974; Susan Bayly, *Caste Society and Politics in India : From the Eighteenth Century to the Modern Age*, Cambridge University Press, Delhi, 1999; Nandini Gooptu, *The Politics of the Urban Poor in Early Twentieth Century India*, Cambridge University Press, Cambridge, 2001; Kancha Ilaiah, "Towards the Dalitisation of the Nation" in Partha Chatterjee (ed.) *Wages of Freedom : Fifty years of the Indian Nation State*, Oxford University Press, New Delhi, 1998; V. Geetha and S.V. Rajadurai, *Towards a Non-Brahmin Millenium : From Iyothee Thoss to Periyar*, Samya, Calcutta, 1998; Rafiuddin Ahmed, *The Bengal Muslims, 1871-1906: A Ouest for Identity*, Oxford University Press, Delhi, 1981; Gyanendra Pandey, *Construction of Communalism in Colonial North India*, Oxford University Press, Delhi, 1992.

40. Sekhar Bandopadhyay, *Caste, Protest and Identity in Colonial India. op. cit.*, p. 2.

41. For more details see, Robert Hardgrave (Jr.) *The Nadars of Tamilnadu : The Political Culture of a Community in Change*, University of California Press, Berkeley, 1969, pp. 200-201.

42. See, K. Aiyappan, *Iravas and Cultural Change*, Government Press, Madras, 1944; K. P. Kannan, *Rural Proletarian Struggles : Mobilisation and Organisation of Rural Workers in South-West India*, Oxford University Press, Delhi, 1988 ; D. Arnold, R. Jeffrey and J. Manor, "Caste Associations in South India : A Comparative Analysis", *The Indian Economic and Social History Review*, 13, 3. July-September, 1976.

43. For more details see, Eleanor Zelliot, "Mahar and Non-Brahmin Movements in Maharastra",' *The Indian Economic and Social History Review*, Vol. III, No. 3, September, 1970 ; Eleanor Zelliot, 'Learning the use of Political Means : The Mahars of Maharastra', in Rajni Kothari (ed.) *Caste in Indian Politics*, Orient Longman, New Delhi, 1973.

44. Sekhar Bandopadhyay, *Caste, Protest and Identity in Colonial India, op. cit.*, p. 3.

45. K. Saradamoni, *Emergence of a Slave Caste : Pulayas of Kerala, op. cit.*, pp. 146-148.

46. Swaraj Basu, *Dynamics of a Caste Movement: The Rajbansi of North Bengal, 1910–1947*, Manohar, New Delhi, 2003, p. 68.

47. Vijay Prashad, *Untouchable Freedom: A Social History of a Dalit Community*, Oxford University Press, New Delhi, 2001, pp. 90-92.

48. *Ibid.* p. 93.

49. *Ibid.* p. 91.

50. *Ibid.*, pp. 164-165.

51. Chinna Rao Yagati, *Dalits' Struggle for Identity: Andhra and Hyderabad, 1900-1950*, Kanishka Publishers, Distributors, New Delhi, 2003, pp. 130-131, pp. 180-181 and pp. 225-228.

52. Saurabh Dube, *Untouchable Pasts: Religion, Identity and Power among a Central Indian Community, 1780-1950*, Vistaar Publications, New Delhi, 2001, pp. 145-150.

53. For more details, see Surinder Singh Jodhka, "Sikhism and the Caste Question: Dalits and their Politics in Contemporary Punjab", in *Contributions to Indian Sociology* (n.s.) 38, 1&2, 2004, p. 180.

54. Mark Juergensmeyer, *Religion as Social Vision:The Movement against Untouchability in 20th Century Punjab*, University of California Press, Berkeley, 1982, pp., 2-3 and p. 74.

55. Surinder Singh Jodhka, "Sikhism and the Caste Question", op.cit. p. 180.

56. *Ibid.* p. 181.

57. Christophe Jaffrelot, *India's Silent Revolution: The Rise of the Low Castes in North Indian Politics*, Permanent Black, Delhi, 2003, pp. 201-202.

58. The reformative movements were further sub-divided into Bhakti, Neo-Vedantik and Sanskritisation movements. In fact, these movements were initiated by Hindu religious and social reformers. By undertaking the reform of the caste system, they tried to keep the lower castes under the fold of Hinduism. In Punjab, the Arya Samaj was against the political movements of the 'untouchables' and opposed the moves initiated for their solidarity and integration. For more details see Satish Kumar Sharma, *Social Movements and Social Change : A Study of the Arya Samaj and Untouchables in Punjab*, B.R. Publishing Corporation, Delhi, 1985 ; also see, Prakash Pimpley and Satish Sharma, 'De-Sanskritisation of Untouchables : Arya Samaj Movement in Punjab' in Prakash Pimpley and Satish Sharma (eds.) *Struggle for Status*, B. R. Publishing Corporation, Delhi. 1985.

59. Eleanor Zelliot, 'Learning the Use of Political Means' in Rajni Kothari, (ed), Caste in Indian Politics *op. cit.*

60. For more details see, Gail Omvedt, The Dalits and the Democratic Revolution, *op.cit.*, 1994, pp. 10-11.

61. Partha Chatterjee has argued that the lower castes often deviated from

the dogma of dominant religions, renounced the Vedas and the Sastric rituals in order to declare a revolt of the spirit. See Partha Chatterjee, "Caste and Subaltern Consciousness" in Ranjit Guha (ed.) *Subaltern Studies VI,* Oxford University Press Delhi, 1989, pp. 203-204.

62. M.S.S. Pandian, "Denationalising" the Past: "Nation" in E.V. Ramaswami's Political Discourse', *Economic and Political Weekly,* October 16, 1993, pp. 2282-2287; see also M.S.S. Pandian, "Stepping Outside History ? New Dalit Writings from Tamilnadu" in Partha Chatterjee (ed.) Wages of Freedom, *op. cit.*

63. M.S.S. Pandian, *One Step Outside Modernity: Caste, Identity Politics and Public Sphere,* SEPHIS-CODESRIA, Lecture No. 4, Published by the South-South Exchange Programme for Research on the History of Development (SEPHIS) and the Council for the Development of Social Science Research in Africa (CODESRIA). Amsterdam/Dakar, 2001, p. 8. and pp. 19-20. This sort of view has also been expressed by Kancha Iliah in his article, "Towards the Dalitization of the Nation" in Partha Chatterjee, (ed.) *Wages of Freedom, op. cit.,* pp. 268-270

64. Michael Moffat, *An Untouchable community in south India,* Princeton University Press, Princeton, New Jersey 1979, pp. 216-217, p. 291. pp. 115-145

65. Robert Deliege, *The World of the 'Untouchables' : Paraiyars of Tamilnadu,* Oxford University Press, Delhi, 1997, p. 13.

66. C.D.F. Mosse, "Idioms of Subordination and Styles of protest among Christian and Hindu Harijan castes in Tamilnadu", *Contributions to Indian Sociology.* Vol. 28:1, 1994, p.68

67. Gerald Berreman, *Hindus of the Himalayas,* University of California Press, Berkeley and Los Angeles, California 1963, p. 224.

68. Owen Lynch, *The Politics of Untouchability : Social Mobility and Social Change in a City of India,* National Publishing House, Delhi, 1969, p. 75.

69. Margaret Searle-Chatterjee, 'Caste, religion and other identities' in M. Searle-Chatterjee and Ursula Sharma (eds.) *Contextualising Caste : Post Dumontian Approaches,* Blackwell/Sociological Review, Oxford, 1994, p. 161.

70. Badri Narayan, "Inventing caste history: Dalit mobilization and nationalist past" in *Contributions to Indian Sociology* (n.s.) 38, 1&2, 2004, p. 216.

71. Ibid.

72. The Hindutva hardliners insist that Bharat Mata represents an ancient concept of devotional patriotism, Vishwa Hindu Parishad leaders like

Ashok Singhal defined the Indian nation as the land of Rama and categorically stated that those who did not respect him were anti-nationalist. Similarly the Bharatiya Janata Party leadership also reinterpreted the Dalit myths, histories and symbols to bring the lower castes within their fold. For more details, see Ibid., pp. 216-217.

73. C.R. Yagati, *Dalit Studies: A Bibliographical Handbook,* Kanishka, New Delhi, 2003.

74. Shalini Ramachandran, " 'Poisoned Bread': Protest in Dalit short stories" in *Race and Class,* Vol. 45, April–June, No. 4, 2004, p. 42.

75. Vinay Bahl, "Terminology History and Debate: 'Caste' Formation or 'Class' Formation" in *Journal of Historical Sociology,* Vol. 17, No. 2/3, June /September 2004, pp. 306-307.

5

Dr. B.R. Ambedkar and the People's Education Movement in India

K.S. CHALAM

The development of education in India as a universal right is considered to be of very recent origin. Though the British are given the credit of being the benefactors of universal education in India, the historical evidence does not support this claim. The argument between Mahatma Gandhi and Sir Hortog is a known controversy in educational history, as Gandhiji could not substantiate his claim that there was universal education in India before the British came to this country.[1] It is equally true that the British failed to provide educational opportunities to every citizen in this country. It was only after the Woods Despatch of 1854, the British Government took some interest in the educational development of the natives. It was again Mahatma Jyoti Rao Phooley who in his memorandum to Hunter Commission in 1882 accused the British for their penchant in providing educational opportunities only to the upper castes, while collecting huge revenue from the illiterate Shudras and Atishudras. One can say that this is the beginning of a movement for mass education in the country. However, no systematic attempt was made by any known leader thereafter for the educational upliftment of the poor in the country. It is in this context, the role of Dr. B.R. Ambedkar as a protagonist of universal compulsory education for all need to be viewed. The universal compulsory education is the "be all and end all" of mass education in India. Perhaps he is the only leader of the pre-independence period who had a vision for a people's education movement to realize universal education for all.

Contextualizing Ambedkar

While contextualising Ambedkar movement as a protest movement M.S. Gore, Gail Omvedt and several social scientists have placed Dr. Ambedkar as a leader of the untouchables. He was never projected by the mainstream scholarship as a positive contributor to the overall social and educational development of the country. He has been a victim of reductionism and in this context some of his followers are also responsible in joining the bandwagon of reductionism. Therefore, one of the important contributions of Dr. Ambedkar to Indian society, the "educational development" has been eclipsed.

It is brought out by scholars now that there were great leaders in South-India such as Ayothidas (1845-1914), Ayyankali (1863-1914) and others who preceded Dr. Ambedkar in their mission of amelioration of the social and educational conditions of the Dalits. But, the contributions of these savants did not attract the all India character, as did Ambedkar. Therefore, it is necessary to evaluate the contribution of Dr. Ambedkar to the mass educational movement in India. It appears that there is no parallel to Dr. Ambedkar during the pre-independence movement in matters of an intellectual input into the argument that the country needed universalisation of education. In this context, Dr. Ambedkar seems to have been influenced by his teacher and philosopher, John Dewey of Columbia University.

Very few Indians in the twentieth century had deliberately chosen to get educated in an open society like the USA. One among them was Dr. Ambedkar and the other prominent figure was Jayaprakash Narayan. Though both the leaders differ in their struggles and outlook, there was a common bondage that could put them together. It was their strong belief in democracy. United States of America at that time was trumpeted as the symbol of liberty and therefore, democracy. There was also a reason for this. One of the prominent advocates of democracy and a great pragmatist was teaching in Columbia University and spreading the massage of democracy through his disciples. It was John Dewey—a great educationist and a democrat. This has perhaps, attracted the attention of Ambedkar and he chose to study in Columbia University. In fact, the formative years of Ambedkar were shaped by the academic atmosphere in Columbia and particularly the lectures of John Dewey.

We will find in the writings of Ambedkar quoting regularly the lectures of John Dewey. We will find in the writings of Ambedkar quoting regularly John Dewey in support of his arguments. Ambedkar got his Post-Graduate and Ph.D. degrees from Columbia, which is even today considered to be one of the liberal campuses in the USA.

Scholars have written elaborately about the contribution of Ambedkar to philosophy, sociology and religion, among other fields. But there are very few attempts by scholars to project him as a great educationist. In fact, more than half of his life was spent in educational institutions. Even while he was in the thick of politics he took interest in the educational programmes of dalits. Out of 65 years of his precious life, he spent around 40 years as a student, scholar, teacher and promoter of education. Therefore, it is necessary to understand and analyse his contributions to the development of education in India in general and to the educational upliftment of weaker sections in particular. In the formulation of special provisions for scheduled castes and other backward classes in the Constitution, Ambedkar seems to have consciously chosen the concept of "educationally and socially backward classes". He knew that those who were considered as backward or uncivilized at that time were the ones who were denied education. Therefore, Ambedkar had been assiduously fighting for the educational rights not only of dalits, but also for the illiterate and ignorant masses of the country. It is unfortunate that experts in education in India seldom recognize his contribution.

John Dewey's Influence on Ambedkar

It is essential that we should reflect here on the educational philosophy of John Dewey. The influence of John Dewey on Dr. Ambedkar is so profound that he himself has declared in June, 1952, after he was conferred an honorary degree in Columbia University; "I owe my whole intellectual life to Prof. John Dewey." This intellectual allegiance of Dr. Ambedkar to John Dewey can be seen in every aspect of his active public life including his social and educational movements. The essence of John Dewey's pragmatism or practical idealism is a projection of the ideal of democracy. His concern is that democracy should permeate every aspect of people's lives including the way people think and philosophize. As Gordon L. Ziniewicz observed that the term democracy for John Dewey is not confined to actual or potential political regimes, but extends to every facet of human culture.[2] Democracy for John Dewey is a way of life, a method of thinking, a manner of approach, a habit of expecting in actively attending to an adjusting facts and conditions as they present themselves. The greatest influence of John Dewey on Ambedkar can be seen in John Dewey's emphasis on the precept that "the people and their relations have to be democratic before democratic institutions can have any meaning."[3] Out of six important works of John Dewey the important book on *Democracy and Education: An Introduction to the Philosophy of Education*, which was published in 1916 had influenced the progressive world including Russia and China at that time. It is here John Dewey said, "Democracy cannot go forward unless the intelligence of the mass of people is educated to understand the social realities of their own time."[4] Education, he said, "is a social process to reconstruction of society." These ideals have influenced Dr. Ambedkar in taking up the agenda of development through democratic nation building. Therefore, many of his programmes including education remained to be the foremost in his agenda of upliftment of depressed classes. Even from the beginning of his political career, he was interested in education.

Economic Aspects of Education

It is necessary to bring here the total intellectual contribution of Ambedkar to the educational development to the mass of people. He is perhaps one of the first economists in the world who had realized the economic importance of education. In his debates in the Assembly and Parliament, on can find the tenor of his argument in favour of subsidies for education in general and for the weaker sections in particular. He was arguing in the Bombay Presidency Legislative debates in 1927 as follows, " We should at least spend on education the same amount that we take from the people in the form of excise revenue. The amount of expenditure that we incur per individual in this presidency on education is only 14 annas, but the amount of money that we recover in the form of excise revenue is Rs. 2-2-9 (Rs. 2.27). I think it is only fair that education of the people as much as we taken from them in the form of excise." He has also calculated the fees income at different levels and argued that it financed 36% of expenditure in collegiate education, 31% high school and 26% middle school education. Higher education should be made cheaper so that lower classes (not necessarily low castes) can enter higher education and benefit from the opportunities it creates. He had lamented that educational institutes were running on commercial lines during the British Raj. His words are prophetic that today higher education became a business that does not recognized 'merit', but only money power.

He was also emphatic in his arguments about the devolution of functions between college and university. He was not at all favorable for professorial positions in the University who do not bother to teach and benefit under graduates. He gave written evidence before the University Reforms Committee wherein he had elaborately discussed the objects of higher education, functions of various committees, etc., which are still relevant. He has also argued in favour of more powers for the University syndicate and also delineated the functions of senate and syndicate in the debates on Bombay University in the Bombay Assembly. He was of the opinion that the object of postgraduate education is to train the student "to learn to distinguish between what may fairly be called matter of fact and what is certainly mere matter of opinion."[5]

Ambedkar was found to be a thorough academic in his approach to problems with practical insights. He has a total understanding of education starting from primary to university level. He has expressed his solidarity vision on research. He spent most of his life for the development of education and even after retirement from active political life, he took interest in the development of educational institutions. He is the first among many Indians who had initiated a people's education movement for the poor.

Legislative Debates on Education

In the Bombay Presidency debates of 1927 and 1928, he raised several issues relating to education, which became important for policy formulations on education. In his memorandum to the Simon Commission on "Concerning the State of Education of the Depressed Classes in Bombay Presidency" submitted on behalf of the *Bahish Kriti Hita Karini Sabha*, he gave numerical data to bring out the miserable condition of the untouchables in the education sector. He has pointed out that enrolment of the dalits constitute 0.87% of the total primary education and 0.14% in Secondary and Zero in higher education. Therefore, he wanted protection for the dalits through education guarantee by making the education of the Depressed Classes as the first charge on the state revenue. He has also projected the practice of untouchability in municipal schools of Bombay where separate *lotas* were given to dalit boys in his budget debates. This, he said, made them to drop out from schools.

In his statement submitted to the Simon Commission on behalf of the Bahishkrita Hitakarini Sabha, he had provided for the first time an authoritative account of the educational under-development of the mass of people in India (The data as presented by Dr. Ambedkar is given in the Appendix Tables). In his detailed note Dr. Ambedkar mentioned that education under the British rule in the Bombay Presidency must have a beginning with the foundation of the Bombay Education Society. It was later named as Bombay Native Education Society and was headed by Mount Stuart Elphistone. But the progress achieved by this society was according to him was minimal. On presenting the data he has pointed out that, "what do these figures show? They show that although mass education was the policy of the Government, the mass were as outside the pale of education as they were before the year 1854 and that the lowest and aboriginal classes of the Hindu still remained lowest in order of education."[6] The lacunae in the British Policy of Education, according to him, was its partial attitude towards the elite. The Court of Director's Report on Education mentioned that "it is our anxious desire to afford to the higher classes of the Natives of India, the means of instruction in European Sciences and of access to the literature of civilized Europe. The character which may be given to the classes possessed of leisure and natural influence ultimately determines that of the whole people".[7] Thus, he found that the education in the British India was confined to few upper classes only. Ambedkar here provided the information and the arguments to show that the landlords, the higher employees and the Brahmins were the real upper classes who were benefited by the British education. Therefore, he wanted that the subsidy given by the British to education, in fact, should provide opportunities to every one of the depressed classes.

Mahatma Phooley was considered by Dr. Ambedkar as his guru and was the first Indian who raised the issue of educational development for the mass of the people before the Hunter

Commission in 1882. It is after four decades later Dr. Ambedkar has provided sufficient data to prove what Mahatma Phooley had brought to the notice of the British in 1882 was right. In fact, as the spiritual heir of Mahatma Phooley, Ambedkar has extended the argument of Phooley by asking the British support for universalizing education. In his debates in the Bombay Presidency he has opposed the introduction of Compulsory Primary Education Act as the proposed Act shifted the responsibility of educating the people from Government to the School Boards. He pointed out that the School Boards would again implement the mandate of the elite as the Boards are dominated by higher classes and with little funding. It is irony that the country is still debating on the free and Compulsory Education to the mass of people even after 58 years of independence. The free and Compulsory Education Bill is still pending in the Parliament for its assent. Even this Bill has several shortcomings, which may not ultimately help the universalisation of education of the poorest of the poor and the Dalits in India.

Ambedkar's Recommendations for Mass Education in 1928

It is instructive here to know what Ambedkar had recommended for the success of compulsory education of the Depressed Classes in 1928. They are as follows:

1. Unless the Compulsory Primary Education Act is abolished and the transfer of Primary Education to the School Boards is stopped, the Sabha fears that education of the Depressed Classes will receive a great setback.
2. Unless compulsion in the matter of Primary Education is made obligatory and unless the admission to primary schools is strictly enforced, conditioned essential for educational progress of the Backward Classes will not come into existence.
3. Unless the recommendations made by the Hunter Commission regarding the education of the Mohammedans are applied to the Depressed Classes, their educational progress will not be an accomplished fact.
4. Unless entry in the public service is secured to the Depressed Classes there will be no inducement for them to take education.
5. In making these comments upon the management for the educational affaires of the Presidency under the Reform in

their bearing upon the Depressed classes, the Sabha is not oblivious to the special provisions made for the education of the Depressed Classes in the form of a few hostels and a few scholarships for higher education. But the Sabha begs to point out that it is useless to make provision for higher education of the Depressed Classes unless steps are taken to ensure the growth of Primary Education. Besides there is no guarantee that such concessions will continue. On the other hand they depend a great deal upon the policy of the particular Minister in charge of education and upon the voting strength of the Depressed Classes in the legislative Council, both of which are uncertain factors and cannot be depended upon."

Constitutional Remedy

Not satisfied with the progress made by the dalits during British in the area of mass education, Ambedkar has deliberately chosen to include the compulsory education for the age group 6–14 in the Directive Principles of State Policy of the Constitution. It is mentioned in the Article 45, as "the state shall endeavour to provide, within a period of ten years from the commencement of this Constitution, for free and compulsory education for all children until they complete the age of fourteen years." It is a matter of great satisfaction to all of us here that the present government is serious in bringing the free and compulsory education Act soon. There appears to be a few weaknesses in the draft Bill that need to be corrected at the time of framing rules. For instances, the definition of habitation in the Bill is not clear as it does not include the dalit *bastis* which are not generally recognized in revenue records. There is also no mention about the opportunity costs of education of Dalit children. In the process of recruitment of teachers as envisaged in the Bill there is no mention about reservations. As the problem of dropouts is basically related to the disadvantaged groups in the rural areas, it is necessary to incorporate some inputs in the curriculum that familiarize and empathize the teachers about the problems of disadvantage.

The people's education movement, which was intiated by Mahatma Phooley, was taken up by his legitimate spiritual heir Dr. Ambedkar. He has, in fact, strengthened the movement with his incessant observations both in the legislative debate and outside.

Like his predecessor, Dr. Ambedkar started the Peoples' Education Society in 1945 to fulfill some of his obligations to the society and to put in practice what he was preaching. His vision for universal compulsory education to democratize not only education but also the Indian polity is bearing fruit now in the form of free and compulsory education Act. This would not have been possible had he not put strategically article 45 in the Constitution. I am sure the Act will become a great tribute to the contribution of Babasaheb Ambedkar to mass education, when it is materialized.

Table-1
Disparity in Education in 1823-24

Classes of Population in the Presidency	*Order in Respect of Population*	*Order in Respect of Education*			*Primary Edu. Students per 1000 of the Pop. of the class*	*Second Edu. Students per 1000 of the Pop. of the class*	*College Edu. Students per 1000 of the Pop. of the class*
Advanced Hindus	4th	1st	1st	1st	119	3000	1000
Intermediate Hindus	1st	3rd	3rd	3rd	38	140	14
Backward Hindus	2nd	4th	4th	4th	18	14	Nil
Moha-mmedans	3rd	2nd	2nd	2nd	92	500	52

Source: Dr. Babasaheb Ambedkar writings and speeches, Govt. of Maharastra.

Table-2
Educational Achievement During 1881-1882

Religion/Category	*Primary Education Enrolment % of total*	*Secondary Education Enrolment % of total*	*Collegiate Education Enrolment % of total*
Christians	0.49	2.26	3.0
Brahmins	20.17	40.29	50.0
Other Hindus	64.69	34.84	22.3

(Contd.)

Religion/Category	Primary Education Enrolment % of total	Secondary Education Enrolment % of total	Collegiate Education Enrolment % of total
Mohammedans	12.54	2.04	1.5
Parsis	1.12	19.66	21.5
Aboriginal and Hill Tribes	0.87	–	–
Low caste Hindus	0.87	–	–
Jews and others	0.12	0.86	0.4
Total	**100.00**	**100.00**	**100.00**

Source: Adopted from Dr. Ambedkar as above.

* * Member, Union Public Service Commission, New Delhi. This essay was originally delivered as a Foundation day lecture of Babasaheb Bhim Rao Ambedkar Central University, Lucknow, 10th January 2006.

NOTES AND REFERENCES

1. K.S. Chalam, 2005, *Challenges of Higher Education*, New Delhi: Anmol.
2. L. Ziniewicz Gordon, *Democracy and Imagination: The Practical Idealism of John Dewey*, www.fred.net.
3. *Ibid.*
4. John Dewey, 1997, *Democracy and Education: An introduction to the Philosophy of Education* (First printed in 1916).
5. Vasant Moon (ed), 1991, *Dr. Babasaheb Ambedkar Writings and Speeches*, Bombay: Govt. of Maharastra.
6. *Ibid.*, p. 10.
7. *Ibid.*, p. 6.

REFERENCES

Ambedkar, B.R., Dr. *Babasheb Ambedkar writings and Speeches*, Govt. of Maharastra.

Chalam, K.S., 1988 *Education and Weaker Sections*, New Delhi: Inter India.

__________, 1993, *Relevance of Ambedkarism in India*, Rawat.

__________, 2003, *Globalisation and the future of Dalits*, Vikas Mumbai.

Durant, Will, 1926, *The Story of Philosophy*, Simon and Schuster.

Gore, M.S., 1995, *The Social Context of an Ideology*, Sage.

Hook, Sidney and Richard Rorty, 1995, *John Dewey: An Intellectual Portrait*, Prometheus.

McDermott, John J., 1981, *The Philosophy of John Dewey*, Chicago.

Omvedt, Gail, 1994, *Dalits and Democratic Revolution Dr. Ambedkar and the Dalit Movement in Colonial India*, New Delhi: Sage.

Zelliot, E., 1996, *From Untouchable to Dalit: Essays on Ambedkar Movement*, Manohar.

6

Special Schemes of UGC for Empowerment of SCs/STs

R.K. KALE

Apart from coordination, determination and maintenance of standard of higher education, the University Grant Commission (UGC) addresses the national concern by introducing the special schemes that help eliminate social disparities and in turn contribute to development of human resources. To achieve the same particularly for SC/ST, the UGC has established special cells in universities to ensure effective implementation of reservation policy, remedial coaching centres to bridge the gap resulting from their earlier educational and social deprivation, special coaching to prepare for NET and entry in services. The salient features of these special schemes and their potential to empower SC/ST are examined and discussed in this paper.

Introduction

The experience of various countries in last four decades has indicated that mere physical and capital resources alone are not sufficient input for developing a nation. Improvement in the quality of people is necessary condition for achieving sustainable and accelerated development (Sudha Rao 2002). Way back in 1961 Halsey, Floud and Anderson suggested that the economies of advanced industrial societies are dependent to an unprecedented extent on the result of scientific research, on the supply of skilled and responsible manpower, and consequently on the efficiency of education system. Therefore, education has been recognized as critical input for economic development, more so-for human resource development.

Japan is one of the small countries which has no sufficient land to cultivate and natural resources for industries. Moreover it was reduced to ashes owing to the dropping of two nuclear bombs only two years before our independence. Its efforts for human resource development yielded desired results to become a developed nation. India is dreaming to be a developed nation. However our huge population is considered to be a biggest hurdle. Since education has tremendous potential to transfer the population into national asset; it could play a crucial role in realizing our dream.

Students in India although learn in the same class but everybody does not come from the same class or caste. Our society is hierarchically structured into castes. As a result the socially disadvantaged groups, particularly Scheduled Caste (SC) and Scheduled Tribes (ST) faced with an intense discrimination and inequalities associated with caste system and untouchability. These were/ are subjected to social, economical and cultural exploitation. This marginalized group constitutes a very large section of India's population, almost one-fourth of its total population. The progress of Japan suggested that keeping such large population of SC/ST socially and economically backward, goes against the interest of the country. Our dream to be developed nation could not be realized without empowering the disadvantaged group in general and the SC/ST in particular. Education is the machine which can generate the power from human capital, to be used for the development of the nation.

Education was historically confined to certain section of society and excluded large section of population making it highly undemocratic in access (Thorat, 2004). Although, concerns for disadvantaged have been shown since long by many, Dr.Ambedkar and Phule remained at the forefront to liberate them from the sufferings due to lack of education. After independence the state made efforts to eliminate the educational disparities. Our constitution enshrined democratization as one of the main objectives of education and anticipated the democratic expansion of education would serve social and economic mobility. Provisions made for social and educational development could be seen in the Articles such as 15(2), 15(4), 17, 46, 335 etc. of the constitution. Different commissions and policies on education in independent India explicitly stated the commitment mandated by the constitution (India 1950, 1966, 1986).

The spread of education among the SC/ST has been slow compared to non-SC/ST communities. Only small fraction not more than 2.4% of the SC/ST student which entered in school manages to go to higher education. The picture is likely to be worse in case of ST. This results into lower presentation in education compare to their proportionate representation in the population. In higher education the percentage of SC students is around 7.5 and that of ST is around 2.5 (Srinivas Rao, 2002). If we consider the enrollment of SC at various levels of the higher education, only 10% and 0.25% go to post - graduate and PhD/DSc/DPhil respectively from undergraduate level (India,1993). Apart from access, to a great extent, there is no equity, equality or relevance in the education system for SC/ST students. The entire education system has been oriented to meet the requirement of one-third of the population, ignoring the interest of the rest (Naik, 1974, Karuna Ahmad, 1979). It is significant that our education system lacks the ability to attract the SC/ST students and retain them. Further social problems are known to obstruct the motivation level, quality and utility of education (Wankhade, 1999). Therefore, the performance of SC/ST students who continue to remain in system and climb academic ladder is expected to be adversely affected. For the academic survival and success of SC/ST students, special schemes are need to be planned and implemented which could attract and retain them in the education system as well as enhance their performance.

The UGC is an apex statutory body for coordination, determination and maintenance of standards of University education. It has always been responsive to the need and constrains of disadvantaged social groups particularly SC/ST. It has been contributing towards social equity and socio-economic mobility and in turn empowerment of SC/ST through the special schemes. These special schemes are likely to retain SC/ST students in education system and help them to enhance their academic performance as well as prepare them for competitive examinations required for services. In the present paper I have examined and discussed the salient features and significance of the special schemes as well as their potential to empower SC/ST.

SC/ST Cells in Universities

The University Grants Commission introduced the scheme of establishment of SC/ST Cells in universities in the year 1983 with the following objectives: *(i)* to ensure effective implementation and monitoring the reservation policy for SC/ST and programmes of Government of India and UGC in universities and colleges, *(ii)* to collect and analyze the data regarding the implementation of the policies in respect of admissions, appointments to teaching and non-teaching positions in the universities and colleges and *(iii)* to take such follow up measures for achieving the objectives and targets laid down for the purpose (X Plan guidelines, 2004).

The SC/ST cell is expected to be active to implement, monitor and evaluate continuously the reservation policy and also to plan measures for ensuring its effectiveness. The UGC provides the financial assistance to make the cell functionally effective. In non-recurring, Rs 50,000/- are given for computer and printer. In recurring, the Commission provides assistance for salary of staff as per actual expenditure (Table 1). Since UGC assistance for these posts created under the scheme is available only for the plan period, it is necessary that a copy of the concurrence accorded by the State Government /or an undertaking by the concerned University in respect of maintenance of the posts after the plan period is submitted by the University to the UGC. Such concurrence is not necessary for Central Universities and UGC maintained deemed Universities getting maintenance grants. Apart from staff salary, UGC provides Rs 1.00 lakh per annum as contingencies to be used for TA/DA for field work, data collection and its analysis and evaluation.

To achieve the objective of the scheme, SC/ST cell circulates Government of India and UGC's decisions and collect information regarding admissions, appointments and training of the members of SC/ST community. As the information on various aspects of education are useful for evolving new or modifying existing policies, it prepares report and digests for onward transmission to various government authorities like the Ministry of Human Resource Development and UGC. The cell deals with representation received from SC/ST candidates regarding their admissions, recruitment, promotion and other related matters. It functions as a Grievance Redressal cell for the grievances of SC/ST students and employee of the University and renders them necessary help in solving their academic as well as administrative problems. In addition, the cell maintains a register for employment of SC/ST in the University and Colleges for various posts. Thus, the cell plays an important role and keeps liaison between the University, SC/ST groups on the campus and government bodies.

The UGC established 88 SC/ST cells till the end of 8th Five Year Plan. Expectedly, the Commission stopped providing any assistance/staff salary to these SC/ST cells particularly in State Universities as respective State Government/Management had given an assurance to take over the financial liabilities with effect from April 1, 1997. Therefore, these cells were supposed to be maintained by the respective University/ State Governments after the end of the 8th Five Year Plan.

During 9th Plan period UGC established/approved 21 SC/ST cells in Universities (Table 2). In financial year 2004-2005, the Standing Committee on SC/ST considered fresh proposals as well as few proposals from the Universities which had earlier been given/ approved SC/ST cells but could not start functioning. The Committee approved the proposals of 13 Universities to establish the SC/ST cells. As a result, by the end of 2004-2005, the UGC was able to approve/establish SC/ST cells in 120 Universities of the country. The year wise working SC/ST cells in different Universities is shown in Table 3. It may be mentioned that there are around 300 Universities in the country. It means more than 50 per cent of these Universities were/are without SC/ST cells. It might be interesting to see how these Universities implement reservation policy and other welfare schemes, and protect the interests of SC/ST without the cells. Therefore, the efforts are need to be made to increase the SC/ST cells in the Universities. It took 22 years to establish 120 SC/ST cells in the Universities. We have to accelerate the work to cover more Universities under this scheme. Moving with the old same speed would be detrimental.

It was quite disturbing that SC/ST cells established during 9th Plan did not start functioning due to non-commitment of the State Government to take over liability of recurring expenditure on posts in the SC/ST cells after the end of 10th Plan period, as the responsibility of UGC of providing grant for the recurring expenditure ceased after the end of plan period.

Meetings/Workshops of Sub-Committee of the UGC Standing Committee on SC/ST have started from September, 2005 in different regions of the country to review the work. In such meetings/

workshops, it came to notice that many Universities were keen to continue or want to establish a SC/ST cell and approached the respective State Government for its concurrence. However, they failed to get the same. It appears some State Governments do not like to take over SC/ST cells after 5 years. These States perhaps think that SC/ST cell is unnecessary financial liability/burden for them. This approach of State Government kills such important programme of the UGC at the bud itself.

In the regional meetings/workshops (2004-2005), the sub-committee (of UGC Standing Committee on SC/ST) also found that few universities are running from pillar to post to get the concurrence of state government. Through hard work and persuasion, one university could get clearance from the Department of Higher Education. Then the matter was forwarded to State Government, the concerned Ministry referred it to the cabinet. The University is now waiting eagerly to know the decision of cabinet. Amazingly, more than two years were wasted for taking this case of SC/ST cell to cabinet. Moreover, not much time is left for the 10th Five Year Plan. It will not be surprise, by the time the University gets concurrence from the State Government and try to establish the SC/ST cell the plan period might be over. In such event, the entire exercise would become futile. Education has always been the state subject. However, after the Constitutional Amendment in 1976 it became joint responsibility of the Centre and State, as education was placed in the concurrent list. With this backdrop, it is difficult to understand the constrains of the concerned State to give concurrence to University to establish the SC/ST cell which is suppose to implement and monitor the government policies and programmes. The lethargy of State clearly reflects the non-sensitivity of State machinery towards the issues and problems of SC/ST.

As mentioned above, there were total 88 SC/ST Cells in universities at the end of 8th Plan. In year 2001-2002, the Standing Committee on SC/ST reviewed the work of these 88 cells which were established up to 31.3.1997. Out of 88 cells, the Committee recommended 46 cells for continuation during 9th Plan (UGC Annual Report 2001-02). It means the function/work of almost 50 per cent SC/ST cells was not satisfactory. Since, SC/ST cells in central universities have been working relatively well, around 28 SC/ST cells remained functional in state universities. We have almost 300

Universities in the country. Therefore, in States Universities the SC/ST cells are either defunct or not established.

An availability/supply of fund is essential for smooth running of the any project and achieving its objectives. The year-wise release of grants for SC/ST cells functioning in different Universities is shown in Table 4. These figures in the table indicate clear trends. Unexpectedly, the grant released for SC/ST Cells was almost continuously decreased. In year 2003-2004, the grant was not released at all, as the revised guide lines to establish SC/ST cells in 10th plan were not finalized by the UGC. It may be mentioned that the 10th Plan period guidelines for establishment of special cells for SC/ST was published and released only in September 2004. In anticipation, the UGC should have taken some interim measures for this period to avoid the non-release of grants for such important scheme. The continuous decrease in grants and non-release of grants in 2003-2004 might have adversely affected the smooth functioning of many SC/ST cells.

Since 1983, the UGC has provided financial assistance to the universities and deemed to be universities for setting up of special cells for the implementation of reservation policy in every Five Year Plan. Some SC/ST cells have done excellent work. The assistance of these special cells, on recurring items, has ceased on the expiry of Plan period. To continue the work in these active SC/ST cells, the UGC decided to provide assistance to each cell to the tune of Rs 1,00,000/- per annum. However, this assistance is only up to the end of 10th Plan period. Although, the assistance given appears to be token, it definitely suggestive of intention of UGC not to disown the SC/ST cells completely at least those have done good job.

It might be mentioned that the UGC has laid down the procedure with many conditions for release of grants (X plan guidelines on SC/ST cell, 2004). No doubt, the conditions are always essential from the administrative point of view. However, these conditions work as brake in smooth running of SC/ST cells. Suitable modifications in the conditions might be useful and augment the functioning of the cells.

For effective implementation of policies and programmes related to reservations for SC/ST, and to ensure prompt disposal of the grievances of the employee of these classes and to scrutinize and consolidate the statistical data, university is required to appoint a liaison officer in the rank of professor and place the cell under him. The university is also supposed to constitute a Standing Committee under the chairmanship of the Vice-Chancellor. It is required to meet twice a year to review the issues and to solve the problems. Thus, through the cells UGC protects the interest of students and, teaching and non teaching staff belonging to SC/ST communities in the Universities.

SC/ST Cell in UGC Office

In response to the recommendations made by the Parliamentary Committee on the welfare of SC/ST, the UGC set up a cell called SCT cell, in January 1979; with a view to monitor the effective implementation of various reservation policies/order on admissions, employment, fellowships, hostel facilities, etc., various programmes relating to access of higher education to SC/ST students and deal with representations received from SC/ST candidates. SCT cell is vital for UGC. The success and failure of various schemes and programmes related to SC/ST depend on its functioning. Since, no details are available about the social returns or impact of implementation of reservation policy/programmes/order; it is not possible to assess the effectiveness of this cell. It must be mentioned that UGC always insists Universities to include a chapter in the Annual Report on SC/ST giving all detail of the activities. The UGC also insists to submit the required data related to the SC/ST. It is clearly stated in the guidelines on SC/ST cells in 10th Plan Period that "if the data is not submitted by the given date, UGC reserve the right to withhold either the Plan or Non-Plan grants until required information/data is received." However, it is quite surprising that UGC does not follow its own guidelines. Although, UGC devotes a separate chapter on SC/ST in annual reports, it just mentions the special scheme and grant released. Surprisingly, no information is provided on enrolment of SC/ST students (state wise, by stage of education, faculty wise, etc), recruitment in teaching and non-teaching positions and their overall percentage, hostel facilities and goals/objectives achieved related to various schemes, in any Annual Report of UGC. Recently UGC has brought out a publication on "University Development in India-Basic facts and figures-1895-96 to 2000-2001" which provides useful data on institutions of higher education, students' enrolment and teaching staff in Universities/

University level institutions and Colleges in the country. Not a single fact and figure on SC/ST is available in this volume. There is complete blackout.

The UGC has completed 50 years of its existence in 2003. It was appropriate time for reflection, introspection and course correction for India's lead education funding organization. For this, UGC published two books in 2003. One book provides a history of the UGC and highlighted various milestones as well as landmark decisions taken (Sharma, 2003). It also brought into focus the thrust areas during the various five year plans and other aspects of higher education.

The second book is a compilation from various policies and planning documents, books, reports of commission, committees, workshops, conferences and panels, highlighting the trends, developments and growth of higher education in India between the year 1781 and 2003 (Kaur, 2003). The book is a result of meticulous research and planning. A separate topic is devoted to disadvantaged groups of society in which some facts and figures related to enrolment of SC/ST students are given. Interestingly, the author has to use secondary data that too from sources other than UGC. Moreover, data is old and incomplete. The fact is that UGC is/was not keen to keep the information and update the same from time to time. The UGC has an Information and Statistics Bureau, which collects information from universities/university level institutions, and colleges every year. However, the UGC has not prepared a document, which gives basic facts and figures on SC/ST in higher education. Without past there is no future the UGC must collect and compile information on SC/ST. There in no need to emphasize on importance of such data for planning and evolving policies.

Remedial Coaching Scheme for SC/ST

The SC/ST students mainly come from a rural background where opportunities for quality education are so limited that weakness in academic performance is inevitable. The weaknesses have to be removed by remedial education and in turn help them to do well in studies. Therefore, the Commission introduced in 1994 one such special scheme namely "Remedial Coaching at the Under-Graduate (UG) and Post-Graduate (PG) level for students belonging to the weaker sections of the society, particularly the SCs/STs."

The main objectives of the scheme are:

(i) To improve the academic skills and linguistic proficiency of the students in various subjects.

(ii) To raise the level of comprehension of basic subjects so as to provide a stronger foundation for further academic work.

(iii) To strengthen their knowledge, skills and attitudes in such subjects, where quantitative techniques and laboratory work are involved, so that necessary guidance and training provided under the programme may enable the students to come-up to the level necessary for pursuing higher studies efficiently.

(iv) To improve over all performance of these students in the examinations.

The tenure of assistance to implement the scheme in universities and colleges is five years but initially assistance is provided for three years, called first phase. The nature of financial assistance available for scheme of remedial coaching for SC/ST is given in Table 5. The period of assistance is linked with performance. The work of centre can be reviewed at the end of third year with the help of Standing Committee on SC/ST and if found satisfactory, further extension of two years would be granted to the College/University. Each University/College is expected to cover a minimum 100 students per year and place the coaching centre under one of the senior faculty members as coordinator of this scheme.

The year-wise position of the proposals approved by the UGC during 1997-1998 to 2004-2005 is given in Table 6. As each academic institute is expected to cover, on average, 100 students the total number of beneficiaries per annum could be at least 10,000 students. It is important that the appraisal reports (For example of year 2000-2001) confirm the scheme as a beneficial to SC/ST students. The remarkable improvement in academic performance (UGC Annual Report, 2001-2002) suggested making all efforts to encourage more and more Universities and Colleges to establish Remedial Coaching Centres for the benefit of SC/ST students.

However, on the other hand, when 202 institutes selected for financial assistance during 1996-97 were reviewed for their work, the UGC Committee recommended extension only for 24 institutes for another period of two years (UGC Annual Report, 2000-2001). Similarly, the commission also reviewed the work of those colleges, which were selected in 1999. The committee could recommend 18 institutes for further assistance in second phase i.e. for two years duration (UGC Annual Report, 2002-03).

During 2003-2004, proposals were invited as per the Ninth Plan guidelines of the scheme. 5 and 113 proposals of Universities and Colleges respectively were selected to establish Remedial Coaching to SC/ST students. However, the UGC did not convey its approval/ sanction of grant to these Universities and Colleges as the guidelines of the schemes for the 10th Plan were at the finalization stage (UGC Annual Report, 2003-04). During the same year (2003-04), progress of the coaching centres approved during 2000-01 was reviewed after completion of the three years. The committee recommended extension of 13 coaching centres for further period of two years (UGC Annual Report, 2003-04).

During 2004-05, fresh proposals were invited from Universities/ Colleges as per X Plan guidelines. The UGC selected 11 Universities and 63 colleges to introduce Remedial Coaching for Scheduled Caste and Scheduled Tribe Students and released grant to them. The grant to 4 Universities and 105 Colleges selected in 2003-04 was released during 2004-05. At present, 15 Universities and 168 Colleges have completed the tenure of three years and review is due during current year at the Review Committee Meetings/Workshops at regional level in different cities. The review is already started from September 2005 onwards.

The above monotonous details, deliberately given here, appear like mere rituals, lacking an academic component to great extent. It could be seen that the large number of proposals are approved and reviewed but the few are recommended for extension. At the same time, as mentioned above the scheme is beneficial and found a remarkable improvement in performance of SC/ST students. In this light, the scheme has to be examined and modified suitably to make it more popular among the Universities and Colleges and in turn more beneficial to SC/ST students.

Table 7 shows the year-wise release of grants for the remedial coaching scheme. This is one of the schemes for SC/ST, which relatively gets maximum grant. Expectedly, the UGC has recognized importance of coaching and supported the scheme liberally. However, considering the extent of need of SC/ST students; the grant is quite small in volume. Moreover, the grant for remedial coaching remained of the tune of around 300 lakh from the year 1997-98 onward till date. Since, the social returns from the remedial coaching are expected to be high, the UGC should have enhanced the grant at least three times more than what it was in year 1997-1998.

A part from above, the UGC also faces problem in implementing the different special schemes including remedial coaching. Universities/Colleges do not submit utilization certificate, statement of expenditure, appraisal report etc. against grant released which causes delay in releasing the next installment. Non compliance of UGC orders/procedures leads to discontinuation of the scheme.

Scheme of Coaching for SC/ST Candidates to Prepare for NET

Despite all constitutional safeguards and measures initiated by the UGC, the position of reservation for SC/ST is far below from the expected level in the Universities even after 50 years of independence. Therefore, in order to provide an adequate number of qualified SC/ST candidates for recruitment as lecturers in Universities and Colleges, the Commission has decided to introduce a scheme of conducting Coaching Classes to prepare them for appearing in the National Eligibility Test (NET), which is an essential qualification for becoming a lecturer in Universities or Colleges. Therefore, as mentioned above the main objective of the scheme is to prepare SC/ST candidates for appearing in the National Eligibility Test (NET) so that sufficient numbers of candidates become available for selection of lecturer in the university system.

The coaching classes could be organized by selected universities for which grant on 100 per cent bases are made available. The UGC is making efforts to allocate at least one centre in each state. The details of grant provided under the scheme during 10th Plan are given in Table 8. There is no provision for appointing of staff on a permanent basis in the coaching centre.

During 2004-05, the first year of introduction of the scheme, 32 Universities have been selected to implement the scheme, for which the Commission released a grant of Rs. 128,000,00/- during the year.

Each university is expected to cover a minimum 100 candidates for each examination to be held in June and December every year. The UGC conducts NET examination in 76 subjects which cover Arts, Humanities (including languages), Social Sciences, Computer Application and Electronic Sciences. In science subjects CSIR conducts NET examination on behalf of UGC. The scheme is for plan period and assistance will be available to the University up to the end of 10th Plan. The university is expected to continue the scheme after commission's assistance ceases.

Since, the methods of instruction/coaching include class work, tutorials and work assignments followed by discussion and face to face interactions as well as formation of study group to help each other, the candidates are likely to benefit immensely and expected to strive for higher level of attainment.

Coaching Scheme for Entry in Services for SC/ST Candidates

During 10th Plan period the coaching scheme for entry in services for students belong to SC/ST community is being implemented through selected universities and colleges to gain useful employment in group A, B & C including Indian Services and State Provincial Services. The scheme of coaching classes for entry in services for SC/ST Students has been introduced by the UGC during 2004-05. The coaching scheme operates at two levels:

(i) coaching for group B & C level posts and
(ii) All India Services, State/Provincial services (X Plan guidelines, 2004).

There is no provision for appointing staff on a permanent basis in the coaching centre. Table 7 gives the details of financial assistance available for this scheme.

During 2004-05, the UGC selected 11 universities and 28 colleges to introduce this scheme first time. An amount of Rs. 86,73,000/- has been released by the Commission for the same. Usefulness of this scheme as an instrument of empowerment SC/ST could be seen after appraisal and reviews.

Teacher Fellowships for SC/ST candidates

The commission had a scheme for "Direct Award of Teacher Fellowships" for SC/ST College teachers by the UGC to do research work leading to the award of M.Phil./Ph.D. degree. Last selections under the scheme were made during 1997-98. Sixty three teachers were selected for the award of teacher fellowship. The tenure of the fellowship had already expired in June, 2001. The scheme has been discontinued thereafter (UGC Annual Report, 2001-02). The year-wise released grants to these teachers during the Ninth Plan period could be seen Table 9.

Many SC/ST teachers were benefited from this scheme. If UGC conducts the study even today it would get pleasant surprises. Large number of teachers from the lot of awardees have contributed to education both in teaching and research. Some have excelled in academics. Few of them are serving the nations in different capacities. This was also one of the schemes whose social returns were quite high. The UGC should have reviewed the scheme carefully before its discontinuation. It is not known what were the constrains of UGC. It appeared that UGC was not serious. It was amazing that no selection were made for the 'Direct Award to Teacher' by UGC during 1996-97 due to paucity of funds. Was it so difficult for the UGC to reallocate/arrange the funds for this scheme? Or was UGC so poor at that time, it even could not financially support the welfare scheme specially introduced for the depressed and oppressed sections of the Indian society. There was also scheme on research associateship for SC/ST candidates. It met the same fate as that of Direct Award of Teacher Fellowship.

Standing/ Monitoring Committee on SC/ST

To oversee the effective implementation of reservation policy in universities, a Standing Committee on SC/ST was constituted by the UGC in 1997. Academic experts, ex-Vice-Chancellor and distinguished persons in the field of higher education, represent the Committee. The UGC has reconstituted the Standing Committee in 2003. The Committee reviews time-to-time functioning of SC/ST cells and implementation of various special schemes and programme for SC/ST introduced by the UGC.

The Commission has also constituted a Monitoring Committee to discuss the problems in implementing the reservation policy for SC/ST in central and deemed to be Universities. The meeting of monitoring committee is organized once in a year.

The Commission has been organizing region-wise (North, East, West and South) meeting/workshop of universities having SC/ST cells to discuss matters related to effective implementation of reservation policy and to interact and share experiences of each other.

The meetings/workshops of sub-committee of Standing Committee on SC/ST have already started from September 2005. Such meetings/workshops were found to be very effective and useful for UGC to implement its welfare schemes. Apart from above, the Committee has been giving several suggestions and asking UGC to take various measures for the empowerment of SC/ST. For example, recently, the Committee suggested UGC to re-introduce research associateship Scheme for SC/ST students and also provide Scholarship to SC/ST students to undertake Post-Graduate studies in professional courses. The Standing Committee has also recommended UGC to hold National Convention to discuss and debate the role of higher education in empowerment of SC/ST. Thus, the UGC keeps watch and control on the universities/colleges through the Standing/ Monitoring Committee on SC/ST for effective implementation of reservations. In addition, UGC also seeks guidance from the same committee(s) on matters related to welfare of SC/ST.

Conclusions

Social disparities are still prevalent. Since higher education is a tool for social and economic equity, UGC has been addressing the national concern of access and equity by promoting several schemes for the disadvantaged groups particularly SC/ST, that help in eliminating social disparities. SC/ST cells are functioning in universities to ensure effective implementation of the reservation policy in admissions, recruitments, provision of residential facilities etc. Remedial coaching centres are being run for SC/ST students for qualifying the NET for lecturership and for entering in services. At present there are 120 SC/ST cells, 136 remedial coaching, 39 for Entering in services coaching and 32 NET Coaching Centres functioning in various Universities (Table 10). From some of the appraisals reports and interaction with university representatives in regional meetings/workshops, these schemes were found to be beneficial to the SC/ST students. Effectiveness of SC/ST cells in implementing reservations was evident from the increased percentage in enrollment and recruitments particularly in Central universities. The facts are suggestive of the potential of these special schemes to attract and retain SC/ST students in higher education system as well as help them to enhance their academic performance and success in examinations related to services. However, administrative handling and not following the UGC procedure/ guidelines often affect the implementation of special schemes, some time leading to their discontinuation. In review committee meetings emphasis should be given more on academic/benefits/outcome of the schemes rather than the administrative procedures. If necessary, the administrative procedures may be modified providing more freedom to the universities which are implementing the special schemes. In vision for 21st century it is stated, "UGC is pursuing a forward looking strategy for development of a human resource which will not only meet the demand for skilled human power but also safeguard the interest of country". Therefore it would be appropriate to undertake systematic studies to find out to what extent the implementation of strategies/special schemes have been translated into social returns. It is possible that the outcome of such exercises might make UGC proud, for contributing to empowerment of SC/ST through higher education.

REFERENCES

Ahmad, Karuna (1979). "Towards a Study of Education and Social change", *Economic and Political Weekly*, Vol. XIV. No. 4. January 27, pp. 158-164.

Halsey, AH, Floud J and Anderson CA (1961). *Education, Economy and Society*. The Free Press, New York, p. 177.

India, Government of (1950). *Report of the University Education Commission*: December 1948-August 1949. Ministry of Education, New Delhi.

India, Government of (1966). *Report of the Education Commission (1964-66)*, Ministry of Education, New Delhi.

India, Government of (1986). *National Policy on Education.*

India, MoHRD (1993). *Selected Education Statistics: 1991-92*, New Delhi.

Kaur, Kuldip (2003). *Higher education in India (1781-2003)*. University Grants Commission, New Delhi.

Naik, J.P. (1974). *Crisis in Indian Education. A search for Alternatives*, Monograph.

Sharma, Kavita A (2003). *50 Years of University Grants Commission*. UGC Publication, New Delhi.

Srinivas Rao, S (2002). Equality in higher education: The impact of affirmative action policies in India. In: *The role of higher education in diverse democracies,* Beckhman, Edgar (Ed.), Association of American Universities and Colleges, Washington DC. pp. 41-61.

Sudha, Rao K (2002). *Educational Policies: Analysis and Review of Promises and Performances.* National Institute Of Planning and Administration, New Delhi; pp. 1-114.

Thorat, Sukhdeo (2004). Marginalized groups and democratization of higher education In: *Challenges facing Indian Universities.* Arun Kumar (Ed.), Collection of Papers Based on a Seminar Organized by JNUTA on October 2, 2004 In Jawaharlal Nehru University, pp. 44-47.

UGC Annual Reports 1996-1997, 1998-99, 2000-01 to 2003-04.

University Development in India – Basic Facts and Figures, 1995-96 to 2000 University Grants Commission, New Delhi, Year 2003.

Wankhade, G.G. (1999). "Social and Educational Problems of Scheduled Castes: Some Critical Insights", *The Indian Journal of Social Work,* Vol. 6, issue 3 July. pp. 399-417.

Table–1
Assistance for the Staff Positions in SC/ST Cell

Positions	*No of Positions*
Coordinators	One
Administrative Assistant	One
Research-cum-Statistical officer	One
Steno-typist/Data Entry operator	One
Peon	One

Table–2
SC/ST Cells in Universities Approved During 9th Plan Period

Year	*No. of SC/ST Cells*
1997-1998	–
1998-1999	7
1999-2000	8
2000-2001	3
2001-2002	3
Total	**21**

Note: Number of SC\ST Cell at the end of 8th Plan was 88.
Source: UGC Annual Report 2001-2002.

Table–3
Year wise working SC/ST Cells in Different Universities

Year	*No. of SC/ST Cells*
1996-1997	88
1997-1998	–
1998-1999	103
1999-2000	–
2000-2001	107
2001-2002	109
2003-2004	113
2004-2005	120

Source: Compiled from the University Grants Commission Annual Reports.

Table–4
Year-wise release of Grants for SC/ST Cells in Universities

Year	*Grants Released (Rs)*
1997-1998	193,59000
1998-1999	50,66000
1999-2000	65,65000
2000-2001	37,86000
2001-2002	42,56000
2002-2003	29,58000
2003-2004	Not Released
2004-2005	13,18703
Total	**433,15703**

Source: Compiled from the UGC Report 2001-2002 and other Reports/Information.

Table–5
Nature of financial Assistance Available for Remedial Coaching and Coaching Scheme for Entry in Services for SC/ST Students

	Coaching For SC/ST (Rs in lakhs)	*Entry in Services for SC/ST (Rs in lakhs)*
Universities		
Non-Recurring		
1. Audio-Visual Aids/ Computer (One)	1.25	1.25
2. Photocopier	1.25	1.25
3. Books & Journals	1.25	1.25
4. Invertor/Generator	0.25	0.25
Total	**4.00**	**4.00**
Recurring (p.a.)		
1. Honorarium to Coordinator	0.12	0.12
2. Renumeration to Teachers/ Scholars	1.50	1.50

(Contd.)

		Coaching For SC/ST (Rs in lakhs)	*Entry in Services for SC/ST (Rs in lakhs)*
3.	Part-time LDC with Computer Knowledge	0.18	0.18
4.	Contingency	0.20	0.20
	Total	**2.00**	**2.00**
Colleges			
Non-Recurring			
1.	Audio-Visual Aids/ Computer (One)	1.00	1.00
2.	Photocopier	0.50	0.50
3.	Books & Journals	1.00	1.00
	Total	**2.50**	**2.50**
Recurring (p.a.)			
1.	Honorarium to Coordinator	0.10	0.10
2.	Renumeration to Teachers/ Scholars	1.10	1.10
3.	Part-time LDC with Computer Knowledge	0.18	0.18
4.	Contingency	0.10	0.10
	Total	**1.48**	**1.48**

Source: University Grants Commission.

Table–6

Year-wise Position of Proposals Approved for Remedial Coaching

Year	*Number of Proposals Approved*
1997-1998	94
1998-1999	90
1999-2000	70
2000-2001	48
2001-2002	92

(Contd.)

Year	*Number of Proposals Approved*
2002-2003	44
2003-2004	106
2004-2005	74

Source: Compiled from the University Grants Commission Reports.

Table–7
Year-wise release of Grants Under the Remedial Coaching

Year	*Grants Released (Rs in lakh)*
1996-1997	227.25
1997-1998	275.00
1998-1999	354.00
1999-2000	277.00
2000-2001	343.00
2001-2002	372.00
2002-2003	284.23
2004-2005	367.73

Source: Compiled from the University Grants Commission Reports.

Table–8
Grant for the Scheme of Coaching to Prepare for NET

A. Non-Recurring		**Rs 3.25lakhs (To be paid in 1st year)**
1.	Computer with printer – (One Set) & Audio Visual aids	Rs. 1.25 lakhs
2.	Photocopier Machine –(One)	Rs. 1.25 lakhs
3.	Inverter/generator (One)	Rs. 0.25 lakhs
4.	Teaching learning-aid material	Rs. 0.50 lakhs
5.		

(Contd.)

B. Recurring	**Rs 5.42 lakhs p.a.**
1. Honorarium (to coordinator)	Rs. 12000/-p.a.
2. Honorarium (to Faculty members for Paper I,II,III)	Rs. 4,50,000/-p.a.
3. Part -time LDC having Computer Knowledge	Rs. 18,000/-p.a.
4. Par time Peon/Attendant	Rs. 12,000/-p.a.
5. Contingency	Rs. 50,000/-p.a.

Table–9

Year-wise Position of Release of Grants to SC/ST Teachers During 9th Plan Period

Year	*Grants Released (Rs in lakh)*
1997-1998	13.13
1998-1999	16.31
1999-2000	17.43
2000-2001	32.56
2001-2002	13.11
Total	92.54

Table–10

Number of schemes for SC/ST in Universities/Colleges in Year 2004-05

Scheme	*Number of College/ Universities*
SC/ST Cell	120
Remedial Coaching	136
Entry in Services Coaching	39
NET Coaching	32

Source: Compiled from the University Grants Commission Reports.

7

Purity and Pollution: Situating the Outcaste Sacred Prostitute in a Hindu Regional Tradition

PRIYADARSHINI VIJAISRI

"The custom of sacred prostitution persisted as a contentious issue for a considerably longer period than other issues concerning women" was a statement made while writing on similar aspects in a manuscript submitted to one of the journal. Its peer reviewer wondered, if it was empirically appropriate, and questioned "Really? Longer than issues like sati that are still ongoing? I think this needs qualification". This bewilderment serves as an entry point to the issues I seek to address in this paper. Extensive research on south India has explored ideological and structural issues complicating the discourse about the ideal of south Indian feminity[1] and specifically those relating to the custom of sacred prostitution. However, inadequacy of historical understanding of the custom, raises serious questions, relating to methodology especially in its handling of cultures at the periphery, communities that are yet to seriously intervene in reconstructing their histories. It is in this context, this paper attempts: Firstly, to locate the process within the 'native' and colonial discourses, transmuted the identity of the outcaste sacred prostitute[2] within a rejuvenated hegemonic resurgence of Hinduism, whereby the outcaste sacred prostitute was lost to historiographical domain. Secondly, it attempts to reconstruct the ritual identity within caste context, and finally to explicate, however inadequately, the mode in which their sacral and impure identity is resolved in mythical cosmology linking to parallels in the ritual and the material realm in the Kannada and Telugu speaking regions.

In Pursuit of the Classical

The nineteenth century witnessed a gradual evolution of the ideal of the 'native' women as a transcendent Oriental construct, whereby various customary practices like sati, female infanticide and early marriage evoked horror.[3] However, it was the custom of sacred prostitution that poignantly reinforced the ideological construct aggregating it by "gross immorality" in the sexually consumed East. Within this abstraction or objectification, the 'Hindu' female itself lost identity while women outside this classical/Hindu frame could almost be ignomible on the lack to amuse the colonial observers in search of the unique, exotic and oriental fantasies. The information generated by the Orientalists, missionaries and official ethnographers provided data for emerging discipline of comparative studies on philology, religion, and culture which sifted the caste Hindu cultures categorized as classical from the 'popular'.[4] In the quest for the philosophical resulting in accumulation of caste Hindu texts in "European libraries a certain contempt for the popular that exhibited crude, primitive and barbarious practices was gaining momentum."[5] This process involved caste Hindus as "native informants and commentators of Sanskrit texts,"[6] who eventually appropriated it in their cultural and political discourses.[7] Perhaps, then it was not an accident that this dispersion of knowledge about the Orient, on "collection, classification and transformation"[8] determined by what was significant for the western gaze was to have implications on the emerging field of Indology and Asian Studies. The custom of dedicating girls to south Indian temples/deities reported by the official ethnographers and missionaries were fitted into evolutionist framework in the emerging discipline of comparative religion that was based on a universal and generalizing framework.[9] The focus can be linked to the colonial fetish for the textual, institutional and 'classical,' customs that could be authenticated by the structural embeddedness and the legitimacy accorded to it in 'high' caste Hindu culture. The custom of sacred prostitution as epitomized in the temple tradition was thus in colonial epistemology, the standard model that could be politically crucial and based on native consensus, not provoking allegations of misrepresentation. Thus, the sacred prostitute simply rendered in early accounts as nautch girl while as a classical model, representative of the hierarchy spatially identified with the Tamil temple tradition of south India. The 'classical' was privileged as the potential site that could be empirically verified, with a rich ideological legacy, as also politically volatile. Further, it had the potential to titillate colonial imagination while simultaneously reinforcing its moral supremacy. For instance, works catering to evangelical organizations and the official circles like Abbe J.A. Dubious, to curious colonial public and organizations orienting colonial imagination like Katherine Mayo[10] to academic concerns like Frazer,[11] Briffault[12] or Farquhar[13] along with the proliferation of travel accounts went into the reconstruction of the classical ideal offering various ideological expositions. Then, perhaps, it cannot be mere accident that the works on the custom have privileged the Tamil spatial unit to the detriment of other geographical entities within the larger cultural unit. [14]

Within this vast body of discrete 'facts' the evidence of 'low caste' 'vulgar' sacred prostitute, structurally ambiguous, failed to evoke interest. Such traditions could logically be subsumed under the notion of aberrations or popular Hinduism. The late nineteenth and early twentieth centuries, western women increasingly interested in issues relating to 'native' women, both political and cultural, enlarged their feminist agenda at home. The nature of intervention determined their perception and interpretation of the oriental women, intermittently producing conflicting views.[15] Actively associating with caste-Hindu reformist and revivalist movements, increasing number of western women were drawn into representation of 'classical' philosophical issues at home.[16] However, the process had to reconcile between nature of native social customs and western ideas. Simultaneously, this knowledge was transformed by active participation and interpretation, disseminated through lectures, associations,[17] and periodicals[18] and fuelled by 'imperial ethos'[19] amounting to ethno-centricism. Even the politically blatant attacks on the custom were fore grounded on the 'observed' facts, that such females were drawn from 'culturally superior' castes like the Brahmins.[20] *Mother India* with a brief and ambiguous account on 'devadasis' within a sexualized colony was acclaimed as the most authentic record of the condition of Indian women. One of the writers noted complained though with great appreciation for exposing the moral essence of the 'natives', "I must put on record that Katherine Mayo in *Mother India*, merely touched on the fringe of horrors".[21] Such delineations were reinforced in contemporary writings, that usually though from 'poor families', girls who were initiated as slaves of God were drawn from 'good caste'.[22] Consequently, the Oriental women depicted the woe stricken upper caste-Hindu and occasionally Muslim women. What resulted perhaps unconsciously was detachment from customs and processes affecting the cultures at the periphery, though moving away from such highly 'evolved' and 'classical' models the missionaries drew attention to the 'popular' manifestations of the custom among the lower and outcaste communities.[23] Interestingly, Abbe J.A. Dubois's sharp observations state a need to distinguish such 'lower' caste women from temple women in the south.[24] However, the rich accounts themselves defy any simplistic derivations, replete with details on rituals and myths. A link between 'popular' and 'classical' was suggested in official ethnography; however, such accounts are structured within rigid and closed cultural spaces not recognizing castes as interacting dynamic entities.[25] The response provoked by such virulent propaganda, ridiculing the sexual personality of the caste-Hindu had to be contained in the politically crucial decades of the early twentieth century by deploying nationalist feminists to postulate a native version of cultural issues so intensely propagated at home and orienting colonial culture.[26] With a measure of success the issue was stalled and reverted by assertion that the custom was confined to a 'minority', it was an aberration and thus not as pervasive as the vicious 'drain inspector's report' had concocted.[27] However, the counter propaganda that resorted to spiritualizing the east in way veiled material realities and institutions affecting the cultures at the periphery. The term *devadasi* embodies this ideological process, legitimized by the native intelligentsia in the early twentieth century, albeit permutations.[28] This was reinforced in the legislative discourses across the region since the early 20th century. The moral victory was symbolized by the passing of the Prevention of Dedication of Devadasi Act in Madras, as the colony was declared independent.

The hegemonic influence of this ideological construct continues to exercise a pervasive influence as historical commonsense as also across disciplinary boundaries. Within this quintessential framework, the devadasi is an ideal, a legitimate historiographical construct determining the course of historical narrative. Works on outcaste sacred prostitution emerged in the region especially within the sociological and anthropological tradition both as sketches and detailed accounts. Based on ethno methodological techniques: field work observer-participant method, surveys, interviews, provided quantitative data bound occasionally by structuralist-functionalist frameworks. In explaining the functioning of the custom, adherence to degeneration or aberration is a dominant ideological trend pervasive as a historical truth. Explication of a 'purely religious institution' as empirically evident phenomenon manifest in the 1980s had to be resolved ideologically. The earliest sketches fore grounded description of the custom on the presumption of chastity, virginity as the pristine value that modeled the proto-type, which eventually 'degenerated' into 'abominable' custom overtime.[29] Recourse is made to several possible trends within the degeneration theory. In its most evocative hypothesis the theory could provide scope for intellectual imagination.[30] Throughout the narrative there is an enthusiasm to trace the crucial shifts from the proto-type. Was it the sanskritisation process that led to a 'confusion' leading to an incredulous mixture of 'old and new tradition' wherein ignorance of 'sanskritic scripts' and historical refusal by the priests to 'tell all they knew' led to a contamination of the pristine ideas in the 'amalgated forms'? Or perhaps, it was an element of 'manipulation' by religious specialists (scholars and priests) along with weakening of Sanskritic religion and coexistence only confounded confusion. Another possibility, 'a ban' by Sanskritic tradition of 'these women' could have reduced them to the 'status of prostitutes'. To look at historically, Muslim intervention transformed them into 'revenue collectors' of state by 'harassing devotees'. With the British introduction of red-light areas, "the devadasis began to move back and forth the shrine" along with "disintegration of feudal setup" sans pomp glory and splendor reduced them to mere "destitutes and prostitutes".[31]

However, departing from the over arching framework is Jackie Assayag whose nuanced perception captures the ambiguous and complex identities of the outcaste sacred prostitutes, though within the general conceptual category of devadasi. As one symbolic of values of renunciation, ideally a Yogamma, but also one of structurally embedded active erotic identity. Though it is at this phase that the issue reaches an impasse in reconstructing the complex identity of the outcaste sacred prostitute. The lack of historical data has fuelled in impressionist, anachronistic and simplistic assumptions in the existing literature. Simultaneously, this has blurred initiative drawing the distinct identity of the outcaste sacred prostitute. Fundamentally, it is inappropriate that the custom that is interwoven with the structural and ideologically, the sub systems within them, the public and private realms, cannot be reduced to over simplistic and ahistorical presumptions embodied, in the theory of aberration. Within this frame it would be a daunting exercise to recover the ritual identity of outcaste ritual specialists, to uncover hierarchy in the myths as also to recuperate the dynamics of inter and intra caste identities.

The World of Sacred Prostitutes

The custom of sacred prostitution encompasses women from various cultural groups, and its linkages with the dominant supra local organizations and its multiple manifestations, emerge as the popular religious custom bringing within its purview substantial groups of women. The tradition represents the interface of caste and outcaste religious traditions and as a religious tradition draws in its fold the dominant Shudra, the lower Shudra and Outcastes.[32] The pervasiveness of the tradition is in its power to draw divinities worshipped by distinct caste and outcaste groups.[33] Within this context—three patterns are perceptible: the Matangi, the Jogati/ Basavi and the Sule/Sani. The caste identity, ritual service, spatial structuring as well as mode of remuneration vary immensely with each pattern unraveling the manner in which an alternative space is cast within the patriarchical caste structure. This context provides scope to understand the complex ways in which caste functions, mediating all types of human relations.[34] The synchronic manifestation of the custom at various socio-cultural foci is expressive of the distinct cultural consciousness in south India.[35] Such reconstruction of the feminine identities within the conceptual category of 'auspiciousness' is typified in the *nityasumangali*. Majority of studies subsume sacred prostitutes manifest in south India within this ideal, a logical culmination of a notion of Shakti, transgressing the profane and exuding the 'psychic unity' of the region. The sacred prostitute, idealized as devadasi, is argued embodies a transcended identity on redemption from caste/shudra identity thus functioning for the universal well-being and prosperity. Eventually paralleling the renouncer, the devadasi, is cast as defying/ countering the normative and the structural values.[36] Given this framework what is overlooked is how caste impinges on the identity of women even within a tradition that, often in idyllic representations, is perceived as conserving trans normative model in contravention to rural structure and life. Such uncritical generalizations fail to account for the complexities within the tradition.

Studies suggest the prevalence of various categories of sacred prostitutes comprising a world of its own yet inextricably bound up with caste ideology. The women share a collective consciousness, a distinct community consciousness, a identity that is transcendent and relatively transgressive – the Jogati/Basavi way of life enacted in the rituals they performed individually and collectively and as a distinct mode of living from the feminine identity rooted in temporal space. Perhaps, the ritual identity of the women has an archetype, the ideal as one who has redemption from temporal obligations inherited by her community, performance of labour.[37] Though majority of women worked as coolies, daily labourers for living, some women said that there was belief, that if these women were employed as labourers the goddess would be angered (Kopa). Jackie Assayag lucidly portrays the distinct persona of the outcaste sacred prostitute as an active ritual specialist; with her, "the coming of the Jogamma can be heard from a far because of the rhythmic tinkling of her bell-adorned anklets similar to those worn by Indian dancers. Her forearms are always covered with green bangles some of which may be made of plants, everything she carries, the decorated basket, the fan made of yak hair (camara) the wicker begging bowl (padalge) is invariably adorned with leaves or branches of neem tree (Azadia chta indeica) considered to be a goddess and to have propitiatory qualities...[38] The Jogamma has a characteristic hairstyle (Jate). Since she never cuts, washes, and combs her hair it is a tangle... she invariably applies to her forehead the red dot (bindi, sindur) symbolizing her status of a married women... another important element of the Jogamma attire is a necklace (muttu) made of red and white pearls...Normally carries two bags on her shoulders. One has two inside pockets filled with saffron powder (Bhandara) and vermilion (kumkum) respectively. The other bag is used as a purse for money and grains, which are given to her as alms. She also carries a one-stringed musical instrument called candike...she wears a green sari symbolizing her power of fertility".[39]

Studies reveal how classificatory models are arbitrary based on a range of notions, ranging from eroticism, ritual functions, sectarian divisions and kinship practices and generally contradictory. Yet they provide a glimpse into the possible models within the custom. The characteristic feature is the classification on the basis of erotic identity and sexual services along with ritual roles. For instance Basavis generally affiliated to the shaiva sect, were categorized as Bala Basavi, Ura Basavi, Jati Basavi, Balagada Basavi, Lingada Basavi, Divatage Basavi, Yade Basavi, Chowri Basavi, Nandi Kola Basavi and Batla Basavi.[40] The Bala Basavis the Batla Basavi transgressed norms of virginity and chastity, "The Bala Basavis...were recruited from the Mahar caste-the untouchables among the Veerashaivas or the Lingayats. The Word Bala means young or maiden. Hence, *(perhaps?)* they were supposed to be virgin and chasteful throughout their life." (emphasis is mine). While Gudi Basavi also known as Ura Basavi functioned within temple and was maintained by it; Jati Basavi dedicated to caste deity whose activities are restricted to one caste; Balagada Basavi 'unique' from other verities as is to 'propagate their progeny' on lack of a male child; Lingada Basavi dedicated to Shiva temples; Nandi Kola Basavi dedicated to 'the flag post of Nandhi, the sacred vehicle of Shiva'. Further, women with specific ritual duties;[41] Divatage Basavi, washerwomen, responsible for cleaning clothes used for ritual purposes and from 'washer men caste - Agara"; Yade Basavi, who is ensured the task of collecting offerings of food from individual devotee families to the deity.

While, according to existing literature, the *jogatis* comprise of a less complex group unlike the *Basavis*. It can at the moment simply be noted that they are classified into *Mangalarti Jogati, Muttukattida jogati* and *kodada Jogati.* The *Mangalarti Jogati* carries the sacred lamp, *mangalarati,* during the procession of Goddess Renuka and generally "attached" to the temple and is in charge of cleaning and oiling the lamp. The Muttukattuida Jogati is a very ambivalent category given the existence of two types of Muttu, the Garati Muttu (beads of a devout wife) and the sule muttu (prostitute's beads) thus and generally is seen as comprising married women, sexually afunctional men, and the outcaste women. Here the identity of the joagti would depend on the type of Muttu worn by the woman though both are ritualized. [42] However, given the confusion and ambiguity regarding crucial aspects of sexuality, functioning and community identity within the postulated models a need to reconstruct the identities of women involved in the regional tradition is evident.

What is virtually made invisible in such constructions is the process in which the organic identity of the women continues to append their ritual identity. In recounting their experiences women found those categories functional in explaining their ritual roles and accounting for several cultural practices. This gains relevance as the tradition drew women form discrete caste and outcaste groups in the region. Though on initiation into a ritual status the feminine identity is transfigured, organic identity remains immutable and functional in the ritual as also the caste complex. The manner in which organic identities are cast in multiplex values needs to be explored. Especially for within this religious complex, spatial access in the sacral as also the temporal space is demarcated for the different categories of sacred prostitutes: the *Maratha Jogati,* the *Mahar Jogati,* the *Holeyar Jogati,* the *Madiga Jogati* or the *Chamar Jogati.*[43]

The Curse of Jamadagni and the Tale of the Two Goddesses

The dominant trend, caste consciousness, within the custom raises crucial issues; the 'origin' of the custom, the rationale for the ritual function of the women, the intricate link between impurity and inauspiciousness, as negotiated in the functioning of the tradition. The textual tradition has little to offer in understanding the syncretic tradition especially its paradoxical fragmentation of mythical plots and characters. It is in.this context that myths exist as an alternative to locate 'origins', on lack of historical data, to locate how "something came into existence, or how a pattern of behaviour, an institution, a manner of working were established."[44]

These myths are embedded in the textual tradition with popular versions, constantly interpolated, are wide spread across the region. Myths synthesize various sectarian plots and values; and ritual enactment simultaneously involved discrete caste groups. Several dominant features emerge in an attempt to deconstruct these myths. However, one distinguishing features in that the myths spread across the regions embody the collective consciousness. This lends scope for dynamism in the mythological tradition to ideologically resolve the contraction in the temporal space.

The predominant myth in the textual and the oral tradition is as follows; Princess Renuka[45] and *rishi* Jamadagni[46] are married in a swayamvara[47] and live in a hermitage on the banks of the river Malaprabha. They beget five sons of whom the youngest was

Parashuram.[48] Renuka as a devoted wife renounces worldly pleasures in service of Jamadagni. Due to her chastity and purity, she gains miraculous powers (Shakti), which are symbolized in the unique manner she fetches water from the river. Those special powers enable her to shape a pot from sand and carry it over her cobra *simbi* (a coil to balance the pot over the head). Once she sees the reflection of a *gandharva* couple in sensuous act and is disturbed (aroused?).[49] On experiencing worldly temptations Renuka loses her *Shakti* and fails to carry water to the hermitage. Jamadagni with his power visualizes this incident and is enraged. Furious Jamadagni commands his son Parashuram to kill Renuka. It needs to be noted that the textual tradition lacks a need to pursue this issue and generally assumes that Renuka revealed enormous powers and was reinstated as the a Shakti goddess. What follows subsequently is crucial, as this sequel of the incident has been a recurrent theme in local caste and outcaste mythology and a space for dynamic interpolations, especially in the oral tradition. This part is subject to contradictions and ambiguities as it deals with constructing the 'other', the 'polluted' within the dominant mythical cosmology.

In Karnataka, according to the oral tradition, Renuka had a female servant, a Matangi (here an outcaste goddess). On orders to kill his mother, Parashuram killed both his mother as well as the maidservant. Impressed by his son's obedience as evident by his matricide Jamadagni offers him a boon. Parashuram requests that his mother be restored to life.[50] Due to darkness the heads of Renuka and Matangi were transposed. Thus, Matangi also came to be respected as a goddess[51] due to this physical interchange. While in another version, Parashuram, who failed to locate the slain head of Renuka, brings the head of a Mang woman.[52] But Jamadagni by his miraculous power was able to reinstate Renuka's lost head. Parashuram placed the head of the slain woman on the hill fort of Mahur and declared that all devotees of Renuka should pay respects to Matangi also.[53] Yet, in another version, a Mang woman, protected Renuka, from the fury of Jamadagni. Pleased by the service of the Mang woman, Renuka declared that the Mang woman will be treated as her younger sister and will be worshipped by the people before they worship her.

One of the myths elaborates the aftermath of the mutilations and charts the course of female tribulations, representing the interface of outcaste and caste religious systems. According to the myth, "Jamadagini flew into a rage, cursed his wife to lose her bodily charms (through leucodermia or leprosy) and repudiated her. Wandering about in the nearby forest she met two Saiva-Natha saints, Ekkinath and Jokkinath, who advised her to take a bath in a pond (Jogula Bhavi) and worship Lord Siva with intense devotion (*bhakti*). They also gave her a round basket (*padalage*) to collect alms. By dedicating herself completely to Siva, Yellamma recovered her former health and returned to the hermitage. On seeing her come back Jamadagni trembled with fury. He ordered his first four sons to cut off their mother's head. Since they refused to do so the ascetic cursed them to become impotent. He then called his youngest son Parashuram who was meditating on the Himalayas. Parashuram accomplishes the task. Pleased with Parashuram's filial devotion, Jamadagni granted him two boons. Parashuram first asked for the boon to restore his mother's life and his brothers' virility. Then he asked his father to expel from his body the goddess of wrath since she was responsible for all the grim events. [54] Similar myth is also prevalent in the Telugu-speaking region. It is said that the slain head of Renuka fell in a house of a Mala and Parashuram by mistake also beheaded the Mala woman. As mentioned earlier the heads of Renuka and Mala woman got interchanged. Jamadagni refused to accept Renuka with the pariah woman's' head, was instead left her to be worshipped by the pariahs.[55] In another version, it is Mathangi who flees from Parashuram on being defeated, conceals her under the tanning pot in a Madiga's house.[56] A Frenchman, Pierre Sonnerat, reported a similar myth in the 18th century from Tamilnad. Renuka is referred by the name of 'Mariatale'.[57] Here Parashuram executes his fathers command "to drag to cut off her head to the place set aside for executions: and to cut off her head. This order was executed but Parashuram was so afflicted by the loss of his mother that Jamadagni told him to go and get her body, to join to it the head that he had cut off, and to whisper in its ear a prayer he had taught him, which would immediately revive her. The son ran in haste, but by a singular oversight he joined the head of his mother to the body of an outcaste women who had been executed for her crimes."[58]

The popular and vigorous outcaste goddess symbolizes this process of cultural hegemony and unfold how issues of identity and sexuality are resolved. The structural location of the 'other' divinities at the periphery makes this evident; be it the existence of Matangi idol opposite to Renuka temple at Soundatti', or that of Jamadagni and Renuka in the village of Tudimille, ten miles to the west of Cumbum in the Kurnool District.[59] The caste identity is inscribed in the myths. Though Renuka is portrayed as a dutiful, meek powerless victim who runs for refugee to the 'exterior', Matangi simply is noted as an outcaste women, servile, insignificant character or even an 'executed criminal', later myths revolve around her. Her active identity is occasionally evident in references to her as having antagonized Parashuram. However, the crucial shift in the positioning of goddess is stated as 'a mistake' that only makes the outcaste goddess invisible in caste Hindu mythology. Thus, this transposition is unwelcome, symbolized in Jamadagni refusal to accept his wife in the polluted form. This physical transformation for the outcaste goddess is crucial as it bestows on her the status of the wives of Jamadagni, gains special powers from the spouse goddess Renuka. This Jogati/Basavi re-enact this by being periodically subjected to widowhood, a tragedy they share with Renuka.

However, the myth also expresses a concern about the uncontrolled feminine, along with the 'other', outcaste women, and fused women. The outcaste woman is a victim with potential of polluting the purity of caste Hindus, though for no fault of hers, contradicts the saga of a Brahmin woman who is tricked into marriage by an outcaste male masquerading as Brahmin, kills herself, "she is transformed into a goddess and in her divine form punishers the untouchable by burning him to ashes or other wise humiliating and humbling him."[60] Renuka on mutilation and pollution is afflicted by the dangerous destitute prowess turns into a monster; only on appeasement by the gods (with special powers to cure small pox) and in restoring her head from the polluted body, is the benign power channalized and structured in its legitimate space, the inner sanctions of the temple. On the contrary, the 'outcaste body' is placed at the door of the temple to be worshipped by outcastes.[61] It is this demarcation in the ritual space that is fundamental to understanding the ritual functioning of outcaste sacred prostitutes. However, the other ritual specialist, Matangi, identified as a 'class of respected prostitutes' reserve a tradition that retains elements of outcaste autonomy and resistance to caste Hindus hegemony in the form of 'ritual teasing' that will be dealt in the following pages. The divine actions organic identity is inscribed and interacts with issues of honour when the erotic element is introduced. For instance, cause for Renuka's beheading is in Jamadagni's incitement on his wife being desired by a Kshatriya, a Kartavirya.[62]

The Rituals of the Jogatis/Basavis

The jogatis, Jogini/ basavi encompasses the caste as also the outcaste ritual space. The notion that women have the power that could be both destructive and benign is central to the identity of the goddess and explains the ritual role of the outcaste sacred prostitute. Outcaste women are bestowed with 'miraculous powers' as in the myths of the popular Arundatti or lesser-known Vasugi. The Madiga female, Arundatti, demonstrates her power to the Brahmin on the look for a woman with 'faith sufficient to transform sand into rice'. "He brought sand and she put it into the pot. He broke iron into small pieces, and this also she put into a pot. She saw what she had in the two pots, but so great was her faith, she proceeded to boil it. With great anxiety the Brahmin stood by and watched. When Arunzodi had finished cooking, behold! One of the pots contained rice; the other was full of curry. Certain that he had found his saviour, the Brahmin waked for Arunzodi in marriage."[63] Similarly, Vasugi, the wife of the Tamil sage and poet Tiruvallur, took sand and boiled it, and it became rice."[64]

Outcaste women are believed to be receptive to miraculous powers through possessions. Such divine visitation is inevitable to control and order the vagaries of nature and appease the destructive potential of the goddess, in an agrarian pastoral economy. Significantly, the role of outcaste women in agricultural economy is crucial, as the outcaste feminine divinity, transforming the dry land into one fertile ensuing prosperity and security in the caste Hindu economy. The description of ritual enactment of the myth, as "sacral primordial events", is to analyze "communal ritual activities", to explicate the manner in which the caste identities are negotiated in collective consecration of rituals. Significantly, it enables recovery of sites of resistance in ritual domain that subverts caste norms and reveals structural conflicts and contradictions. The apodictic power of the myths is evident by the outcaste sacral specialists who in the ritual performance enter, along with their lay devotees, 'a transfigured, auroral world impregnated with the super naturals presence.'[65] However, this attempt makes no pretensions to a systematic and theoretical approach to study of rituals of the outcaste sacred prostitutes. Interpretations are strictly limited, both in the selection of rituals and also analysis recognizing the complexity inherent in the religious experiences of devotees from various caste groups and in the regions. I have only drawn from interviews with the ex-Jogatis and ex-Basavis in Raibag and Ghattaprabha taluk in Belgaum district conducted recently.

Distinct models of ritual behaviour orient women across caste and outcaste communities. For instance, the spouse goddess Renuka is predominantly worshipped by caste Hindu women, while Matangi or Yellamma guides the outcaste sacred prostitute who performs ritual roles as a representative of the goddess. In the periphery of caste Hindu ritual tradition, the Matangi (a Madiga woman) identified as a priestess, a class of respected prostitute representing an antagonistic ritual tradition. The significance of the Jogati/Basavi tradition is embedded in the ritual roles, performed by the ritual specialists as integral to religious ceremonies of household, the temple and the village, an agrarian economy, at the mercy of unpredictable powers of nature. Rituals and festivals are often prelude to agricultural operations.[66] And it is in this context that they were "traditionally indispensable for conducting important rites to propitiate the goddess" as the priestess of the goddess.[67] The ritual roles of the Jogatis/Basavis clearly figures in the rituals and gains legitimacy for the power she embodies as representative of the goddess Yellamma. Symbolic of auspiciousness, their presence during domestic ceremonies and festivals is marked, 'to bestow good crops, promote human and animal fertility as well as welfare of the whole community."[68]

On auspicious and significant ceremonies like marriage and *gruha praveshams* (house warming ceremonies) their presence is believed to exude ritual auspiciousness with the potential to contain inauspiciousness. On such occasions caste Hindu devotees offer worship to the goddess in the jaga of the jogati/basavi and circumnutates it while the latter sing, recite mantras or slokams to the goddess and anoint them with bhandar on the forehead, to ensure blessings of Yellamma. During house warming ceremony, the presence of Jogati/Basavi is believed to 'absorb all evils' in other words, while also the Devara torodu event, getting the goddess home.

Caste Hindu devotees/women on return from visit to Yellamma temple solicit Jogati/Basavi for Jagran on the event of offering ambil (a sweet dish) and prostrate on their feet for being the representative of the dreaded goddess. This specific ritual event is known as Ambil Vidhi.[69] Similarly, another interesting event is the *Measla Utta*. Associated with rituals related to cattle breeding to ensure fertility and productivity, that has reproduced. A group of Jogatis are invited on the 5th day of reproduction/breeding and offered Nivedya (consecrated food offered to gods) of ghee/clarified butter of milk of that animal, collected for 5 days, in ritually pure form. While the Jogati sing praises of the goddess, they are propitiated, the caste Hindu women prostrates the jogatis/basavis and offer them food in the rooms hosting the god/deity (devara mane). Similarly when caste Hindu devotees, the Gowda, Lingayat, seek blessings of the goddess to avert personal calamity or undertake to fulfill a vow, the Jogati/Basavis are applied for. The devotees visit the hamlets of Jogatis/Basavis and inform them of their religious vow and along with a group visit the goddess and propitiate her. Another interesting ritual presence was mentioned relating to agricultural operations is the occasion of digging a well prescribed with offering worship to the gods/goddess. The Jogati/Basavis were called in for their ritual services to accomplish the task.

The Jogati/Basavi performs active roles during rituals concerning the village community too. During the fairs and festivals it is in the form of propagating the omnipotence of the goddess, application of vermilion and turmeric (Bhandar) as sing of auspiciousness and participation in its *pujas*, to mediate ritual activities of the devotees and the priests at the temple.[70] *Okkali* is another ritual event, connected to rain rites, that has resonances with the *jala krida* performed in Orissa,[71] especially as the region is drought prone. This practice assumes variations in the region. While Jogati/Basavi women noted that it was associated with dombar caste women dedicated to Hanuman. The involvement of Jogatis or Basavis is documented by studies undertaken in the 1980s. Jatratkar observes that the okkali was prevalent in Soundatti and Ramdurg taluks. Its villagers celebrate Hanuman Jayanti on the full moon day of Chaitra in a peculiar way. They dig a small ditch and fill it with muddy water. The males in the villages along with the Devadasis come in procession to the ditch. The devadasis are asked to stand around the ditch and the so-called respectable persons throw the muddy water on the devadasis. The devadasis pretend to beat them with small sticks. This play (called as Okkali is local parlance) goes on for some time until the eyes of the males are satisfied to look at the wet bodies of the young devadasi. In return to this 'enjoyment' each devadasi gets about 10 to 20 rupees. The villagers strongly defend the custom of devadasi and insist on dedications pointing out that the above 'religious' tradition must be maintained.[72] However, Tarachand describes it as interwoven with the celebration of holi festival. It is noted that the Jogati/Basavi sing erotic songs and performs 'obscene' dances in celebration that linger on till late night.[73] Their distinct ritual role is in the 'a game' of *holi habba* (holi festival) when the gods are brought from the temple to officiate the event, "the cement walled pit (*okkali gundi*) located in front of the temple of Virabhadra; is dug and cleared. Later the youth fill this with water colour powder and worship. The village deity is brought in a palanquin and sealed at one edge of the pit. New earthen pots provided by the village potters are fitted with the coloured water and placed around the pit and worshipped. By this time the youth come scantily dressed and prepared to play colour. They sit at one edge of the pit facing the deity and worship both the deity and the pots. They are given ritual material and asked to get up there. Meanwhile the devadasis in the village come in a group and accompanied by pipe music to play colour. They are also made to sit at the pit and receive ritual materials. Now the youth are on one side and the devadasis on the other. These two groups play colour, making the devadasi as the target. As the youths approach to pour coloured water on them from the pot they try to escape by running here and there. They even try to snatch the pot and pour coloured water in it on the youth. This often results in bodily tussle... the sport goes on till all the coloured water in the pit is used up. Later the participants go to the village tank for ritual bath. After the ritual bath they visit the temple of the village deity for a worship, before they go home."[74]

Interestingly, the women were held to have mysterious powers to prophesize and their ability to forecast human and natural events is greatly recognized. For instance B.R Patil notes, " these women were reputed to prognosticate events such as rain, weather, crops, etc., in which the village people were interested. On the first day of the Hindu calendar- the *Yugadi*- they used to worship the musical instrument guitar-, which they used to carry with them wherever, they went. They used to go from house to house foretelling the events and collecting gifts while playing the *Tamburi*."

Auspiciousness and Impurity

Jogati/Basavi, as representatives of the goddess (find an affinity with the Matangi, the Yellamma who is inferior to the spouse-goddess Renuka) perform their roles in conformity to the dominant structural norms; crucially the manner in which food is handled in such communal interactions makes this evident. The women were generally held with veneration and not served impure food or the leftovers generally offered to outcastes they believed that such action would enrage the goddess. However, according to Jogati / Basavi carry their own utensils (if disposable banana leaves used for serving food were not used) to participate in a feast hosted by caste Hindu devotees. If the community of jogatis / basavis' were hosted the outcaste women were bound by spatial demarcation of segregation, the touchable jogatis's maintaining a ritual distance from the outcaste jogatis. Similarly, interaction is modeled enabling collective interaction patterned by norms of purity/pollution as in 'ritual distance'.[75] Further, food with potential for 'internal pollution' is ritually managed by containing it with offering made in utensils belonging to the women. Thus, activities are subject to graded interaction between multiple castes interacting with specific roles in the accomplishment of the rituals. Offerings unlike of money, cloths or grains, like cooked food made on their begging rounds (Jaga bedodu) is not like that offered to priests.

Similarly, the outcaste goddess suffers a greater 'humiliation,' Matangi is transfigured from a dynamic goddess to one humbled and inferior not only to the caste Hindu divine actors but their devotees too, in issues concerning purity/pollution in the caste Hindu mythological cosmology. David Kinsley notes the 'unique' manner in which devotion to the goddess is expressed due to her intrinsic impure identity, "Normally, Devotees are careful to offer particularly pure food or food that the deity especially likes. After the deity has eaten it (consumed its spiritual essence) the food is returned to the worshiper. This leftover food (*accost*, although it is not called this) is referred as *prasada* (grace) The ritual give -and – take in this case emphasizes the inferior position of the devotee, who serves the deity and accepts the deity's leftover food as something to be cherished. In the case of Matangi, worshippers present her with her own highly polluted leftover food and are themselves in a state of pollution while doing so. In one case, a devotee offers Uccista-Matangini a piece of clothing strained with menstrual blood in order to win a boon of being able to attract someone. Menstrual blood is regarded in almost all Hindu texts and contexts as extremely polluting, and menstruating women are forbidden to enter temples or otherwise serve the deities. In the case of Matangi, these strict taboos are disregarded. Indeed, are flaunted."[76] Outcastes' access to resources and spaces in the public realm was denied and condemned is evident by ethnographic studies conducted in the early decades of the postcolonial period. Similarly, the spatial segregation and strict adherence to ritual distance in interactions at various levels was pronounced.[77] Perhaps the sacred prostitute could not be left to transgress the caste norms and models of behaviour.

Sites of Dominance and Subversion

Outcaste religion, as documented since the nineteenth century, was predominantly associated with violent ritual practices, unlike the caste Hindus. Perhaps the extraordinary physical and mental powers exhibited by the outcastes could have had a poignant effect shattering the illusionary barriers of cultural indifference terrifying the 'outsider'/the oppressor. A logical consequence would be that on being overwhelmed the 'outsider' sought to acknowledge the supernatural elements and co-opt it. Within such context the act of interpolation is a process beset with complexities, ambiguities and contradictions. The appropriation of outcaste ritual specialists within caste Hindu tradition could be symbolic of the process of caste hegemony. It needs to be noted that the outcaste sacral tradition continues to periodically reinforce the omnipotence of the outcaste goddess and its ritual specialists within the caste complex and subverts the caste values.

In a parallel alternative ritual setting the rules and motives are antagonistic to the one generally represented by Jogati/Basavi in Karnataka. The goddess Matangi is represented by, a representative names after her Matamma/Matangi, humbling, mocking the caste Hindus and virtually dares to pollute them and shatters their claims to superiority. During initiation rites as also village festivals, for the *gramadevtas*, the Matangi acts as a divine mediator, recreating the vigour and terror of the dreaded goddess, "who is aroused, hot and fierce"[78] whose spirit possess her; She runs about among people, touching them with her stick, spurting toddy from her mouth all over them, and backing up against higher castes, even Brahmans, stand in line, as anxious to be spat upon and touched by her stick and her person as are the lowest.... as she rushes about spitting on those who under ordinary circumstances would almost chose death rather than to suffer such pollution. From a Madiga, she breaks into wild, exulting songs, telling of the humiliation to which she is subjecting the proud caste people. She also abuses them all thoroughly, and as in the worship of Bangaramma, they appear to accept it and not to be satisfied without a full measure of her invective.

After this ceremony she visits the homes of the Brahmans, and her visit does not appear to be a pleasant one for them. She comes into the courtyard and smears a pot with cow-dung, on which she places her basket. The inmates of the house at once fill the basket with food and cover the top with a layer of powdered rice. Then a small lamp is placed on top of this and lighted. This appears to be the nearest approach to worship the Matangi receives. She then holds out a pot and asks for toddy. Water is usually brought instead and filling her mouth with this she again goes through the process of spattering them all. The women give their bodies, and the head woman gives her the cloth, which she is wearing. The men give her their scared threads, she then leaves the place, still singing her wild songs telling of the humiliation to which she has reduced the Brahmans.[79] The ritual sacrifice of the buffalo prevalent through out the southern country preserves such religious tradition.

A male buffalo, called Devara Potu/Gajam Pothu i.e. devoted to the goddess, is brought before the image and its head cut off by the head Madiga of the town/village.[80] The blood is caught in a vessel and sprinkled over boiled rice, and then the head, with the right foreleg in the mouth, is placed before the shrine on a flat wicker basket, with rice and blood on another basket just below it." In some places, "Its neck is placed over a small pit, which has been dug to receive the blood, and entrails are taken out and placed in a pit with the blood. Their right leg is then cut off below the knee and put cross wise in the mouth, some fat from the entrails is placed on the forehead and a small earthenware lamp about as thick as a man's two hands, with a wick as thick as his thumb, is placed on the fat and kept there lighted, till the festival is over. Some of the blood and the entrails are then mixed with some boiled rice and placed in a new basket, with a Madigas, stripped naked, places on his head and takes them round the boundary of the village fields, accompanied by a washer man carrying a torch, and followed by a few of the villagers. He sprinkles the rice, blood, and entrails all round the boundary".[81] A More frenzied and violent acts could follow other animal sacrifice, for instance that of a lamb is mentioned as follows, "the intestines of the lamb...are put over the neck of a Mala, and its liver is placed in his mouth, while another Mala takes the basket rice soaked in blood and mixed with the entrails of the buffalo. A procession is then formed with these two weird figures in the middle. The man with the liver in his mouth is worked up into a state of frantic excitement and is insured by the goddess. He has to be held by men on either side of him, or keep fast with ropes, to prevent him rushing away; and all around him are the *ryots, i.e.*, the small farmers, and the Malas, flourishing clubs and swords, and throwing limes into the air, to drive away the evil spirits. As the procession moves through the village, carries the basket sprinkles the rice soaked in blood over the houses to protect them from evil spirits, and falls down in a faint."[82] Elmore mentions a similar practice, "After the sacrifice of a buffalo has been accepted by Bangaramma, people dance like demons while the drums and horns keep up the wildest din. A strange custom is now observed. The Madigas, who are outcastes, begin to revile caste people, using the vilest language. They certainly are adepts at invective, and make good use of their opportunity. The caste people not only accept this berating, but they demand it. If the Madigas show any reluctance to begin caste people will beat them with ropes and sticks to compel them to perform their duty.

The outcaste ritual specialist across the southern region is integral and parallel to dichotomous religious traditions. The ritual identity of the incorporated and the dynamic archetype emerge as models to delineate the manner in which feminine identity is integral to caste Hindu cultural hegemony and its implications on cultures at the periphery of caste society yet the basis of caste economy. What is discernible is the fact that the ideal of outcaste ritual specialist incorporated in caste Hindu tradition is transfigured to reinforce caste Hindu cultural hegemony. This is explicit in the process by which the outcaste ritual specialist functions primarily for the security, prosperity and stability of caste society by propagating beliefs that are contested in her primordial tradition. Thus structural conflicts generate narratives of contestation embodied within the oral so also the textual tradition interwoven with the crucial process of cultural hegemony by the dominant caste groups, manifesting in the ritual realm. Suzanne Hanchett, in similar ritual interludes between caste Hindu communities, notes that ritual teasing or ritual battles... can also be seen as expressing certain types of conflicts or contradictions in the social structure."[83] While the archetypal model within the temporal constraints succeeds in reiterating its autonomy by the capacity its ritual specialists exhibit in performing violent, frenzied rites that violate caste ideals and ridicule them by extraordinary feats. Within this regional context the outcaste ritual specialists, conserve this tradition, ritually strip the Brahmins/caste Hindus off their superiority, which is eventually proclaimed by exultation. This ritual stripping symbolizes the impotence of caste Hindu norms and the invincibility of the outcaste goddess. In its subversive and resistive potential that the ritual events emerge meaningful, that could release tensions, negotiate conflicts and thus are empowering, in howsoever-limited sense, in the temporal sphere. In this space the outcastes reenacts their identity and extraordinary capacity and the Brahmin, the Shudras cannot but acknowledge it from a distance. Though it is eventually by resorting to purificatory rites that the caste Hindus reaffirms their superiority. It is at the periphery that the conflicts prevail and in eventual appropriation that their subversive potential defused. To the dominant class such activities reveal periodically the dangerous implications of such physically overpowering and powerful expressions if transposed in the temporal sphere.

Caste norms constitute the fundamental principle patterning the ritual identity of the Jogati/Basavi. Within the multiple contradictory hierophanies in the myth two notions emerge prominently. The unchastity of caste Hindu wife is potentially destructive that signals disease, drought, and chaos while the erotic identity of the outcaste women, legitimize her ritual interventions, could reinvigorate the passive elements of nature and ensue prosperity and stability. Stridharma and Jatidharma are complexly interwoven and the notion of feminine dynamic principle of Shakti seeks not to transcend them but negotiate them and where non-negotiable ambiguity, as sacral mysteries, exists to the detriment of those at the margins of such traditions. Stridharma then is defined, in this context, by one's organic identity and thus while the mutilated Matangi, for inevitable fatalistic event of 'mistake,' could be subsumed with loss of identity, the Brahmin woman tricked by a outcaste into marriage on discovery of actual identities, legitimately, destroys her children and husband and curses him to be born as a buffalo and burns herself.

Conclusion

The Jogati/Basavi in her ritual identity strikingly transgresses the temporal norms, at once transcending the caste Hindu wife in representing the dynamic feminine principle. This liberative dimension, however, is constrained by the norms of purity and pollution orienting collective ritual enactment. Perhaps, though the religious notion of auspiciousness is in conjunction with that of the pure and impure working simultaneously in harmony with importance to rework or transfigure the temporal space. This paradox is exhibited by prostration and strict adherence to ritual distance as "involuted" or "multiplex" principles.[84] The Jogati/Basavi is recognized as a feminine ritual specialist, an active feminine principle par excellence in the sacral time and sacral space. In re-enacting the sacral primordial events she gains powers that are sacrosanct and functional in regenerating life ensuing fertility, prosperity and stability. Yet, ritual distances according to caste norms of interaction dictate ritual behaviour, empowering the caste Hindu woman who retains her purity to ensure the sacrosanctity of the household. The *jaga*, that hoists the goddess, resolves the conflict between auspiciousness and impurity by redeeming her of a hierarchised or structured role within the temple.[85] Similarly, the mode of paying for their services is resolved by synthesizing caste practices, offerings in return for their services in the form of cloth, grain, and money and cooked food.[86] This practice was not unconventional, as outcastes 'right' to begging for food on festive and other occasions have been reported in both Karnataka and Andhra Pradesh.[87] Customary begging or collecting offerings from household for their livelihood effectively reinforced their identity and rendered them vulnerable in an immutable oppressive structure.[88] The caste Hindu woman and the outcaste women interact and accomplish their ritual roles not in transgression of the structural norms. What is of crucial relevance is that the hegemonic values when legitimized by state, through interventions, impinge on community identities that have resuscitated in postcolonial phase.[89] Especially, of relevance is the manner in which state addresses cultural issues involving sexuality and community identity in this context. Such structural realities challenge the modernist agenda of the postcolonial state, and its repressions, representations and ruptures with the cultures at the periphery. In this backdrop academic investigation of regional traditions based on oral traditions, integral to literal and non-literal cultures entails employing a methodology that synthesizes historical and anthropological approaches. In such complex societies theorization and grand narratives often seek to privilege the hegemonic, normative and the textual, uncritically. The term archive, as in feminist history, needs to be reconfigured to move beyond it to engage in a dialogue with the folk, the field and the actor. Only such a syncretic approach, committed to recovering the voice and experiences of the cultures at the periphery of caste societies, would enable understanding a living tradition oriented by its 'local' rationality, notion of time and sensibility.

Acknowledgements

I am grateful to all the ex-Jogatis and ex-Basavis who cooperated, not complaining about my frequent visits to their hamlets, often coinciding with their working-hours and for sharing their experiences. Especially Sushila Naik, Mala Sane, Vina Mane, Ellavva K., and the staff at the Myrada office, Ghattaprabha. As usual Dr. N.D. Jatrakar (nee N.D. Kamble) has been always been kind, sharing his ideas and introducing me to people and institutions. Prof D.L Seth with his generous comments and Prof. Suresh Sharma with his constant support, have been great source of encouragement. Much of the data in the paper was drawn from the fieldwork carried out in Kannada speaking regions intermittently during 2004 to 2005. I am grateful to the Dr. K.R. Narayanan Center for Dalit and Minority Studies, Jamia Milia Islamia for their interest in publishing my work.

NOTES AND REFERENCES

1. George Hart, "Women and the sacred in ancient Tamilnadu", *Journal of South Asian Studies*, vol. 32, (1973); Susan Wadley, *The powers of Tamil Women*, (New York, 1980); Vijaya Ramaswamy, *Walking Naked: Women, Society, Spirituality in South India*, (Shimla, 1997).
2. The custom of dedication among outcaste communities was popular religious practice in the Kannada and the Telugu speaking regions intermittently acknowledged by media reports till a decade ago. Journalists, activists and reform and rehabilitation agencies vociferously

debate instances of dedication. The state government issued the Prohibition of Dedication Act (1982 in Karnataka and in 1988 in Andhra Pradesh) initiating a state sponsored rehabilitation programme that became effective only in the 1990s in certain pockets of the region only.

3. Information on the oriental women had poured in from various quarters, and by the "1890s discussion of the "position of Indian women" had become so formulaic that one writer feared", there is perhaps danger of... (the public) becoming wearied by a too frequent repetition of the story" as mentioned in Antoinette M Burton, "The White women's Burden British feminists and "the Indian Women", 1865-1915" in Nupur Chaudhuri and Margaret Strobel (ed.), *Western Women and Imperialism Complicity and Resistance*, (Bloomington and Indianapolis, 2001), p. 147.

4. For instance Max Muller, *Natural Religion*, (Delhi, 1979), (first Published in 1889), also see P.J. Marshall, *The British Discovery of Hinduism in the Eighteenth Century*, (Cambridge, 1970); Nancy G. Cassels, (ed.), *Orientalism, Evangelicalism and Military Cantonment in Early Nineteenth Century India: A Historiographical Overview*, (Queenston, Canada, 1991).

5. These views circulated across travelogues and missionary accounts.

6. Gauri Viswanathan, "Colonialism and the Construction of Hinduism" in Gavin Flood (ed.), *The Blackwell Companion to Hinduism*, Blackwell Publishing, p. 16.

7. *Ibid.*, p 17

8. Bernard S. Cohn, *Colonialism and its form of Knowledge*, (OUP, 1996), Introduction.

9. James Frazer *Adonis, Attis, osiris*, (London, 1907), Robert Briffault, *The Mothers: A study of Origins of Sentiments and Institutions*, 3 vols., (London, 1927).

10. Katherine Mayo, *Mother India*, (London, 1927); and *Slaves of the Gods*, (London, 1929).

11. James Frazer, *Adonis, Attis, Osirs*, (London, 1907).

12. Robert Briffault, *The Mothers: A Study of Origins of Sentiments and Institutions*, 3 vols., (London, 1927).

13. J.N. Farquhar, *Modern Religious Movements in India*, ((Delhi, 1967), (first published in 1914).

14. For instance, Saskia Kersenboom-Story, *Nityasumangali: Devadasi Tradition in South India*, (Delhi, 1987). Also see her article "The Tiruttani Temple Dancers" in Jula Leslie (ed), *Roles and Rituals for Hindu Women*, (Delhi, 1992); Amrit Srinivasan, "Reform or Continuity?: Temple Prostitution and the Community in the Madras Presidency", in Bina

Agarwal (ed.), *Structures of Patriarchy: State, Community and Household in Modern Asia,* (New Delhi, 1988); S. Anandhi "Representing Devadasis: Dasigal Mosavalai as a radical text", *Economic and Political Review,* Vol. XXVI, Nos.11-12, (1990); Kalpana Kannabiran, "Temple women in South India: A study in Political Economy and social History", Un published Ph.D. Thesis, Jawaharlal Nehru University (1992) and her article "Judiciary, social reform and debate on 'Religious Prostitution" in Colonial India", *Economic and Political Weekly,* Vol.30, No. 43,(1995); Janaki Nair, "The Devadasi, Dharma and the State", *Economic and Political Weekly,* vol. 29, No. 50, (1994). Leslie C. Orr, *Donors, Devotees and Daughters of God: Temple women in Medieval Tamilnadu,* (New York, 2000).

15. Association of western women with Brahma Samaj members and activities in juxtaposition to missionaries like Emma Rouschenbough-Clough, actively associated with outcastes of the Telugu speaking region, debunked the monolithic construction of oriental women.
16. For instance see the representation of the 'Devadasi custom' in theosophical movement and its influence both in south India as also in the west.
17. For instance, the establishment of the National Indian Association in England by Mary Carpenter to disseminate knowledge about the colony, as mentioned by Barbara N. Ramusack, "Cultural Missionaries, Maternal Imperialists: British Women Activities in India, 1865-1945", in Nupur Chaudhuri and Margaret Strobel (eds.), *Western Women and Imperialism: Complicity and Resistance, op. cit.,* p. 122.
18. See, *The Englishmans' Review, Women's Suffrage Journa*l that reprinted 'native' excerpts from the *Madras Mail,* and *Women's Penny Paper, The New Statesman.*
19. Antoinette M. Burton, "The White Woman's Burden: British Feminists and 'The Indian Woman', 1865-1915", in Nupur Chaudhuri and Margaret Strobel (eds.), *Western Women and Imperialism: Complicity and Resistance,* (Bloomington and Indianapolis, 2003) p. 138.
20. Katharine Mayo, *Mother India, op. cit.*
21. Henry J. Greenwalk, *Storm Over India,* (London, 1930), p. 253.
22. Amy Carmichen, p. 258.
23. Henry Whitehead, *The Village Gods of South India,* (Calcutta, 1921).
24. Abbe J.A. Dubois, *Hindu Manners, Customs and Ceremonies,* (Translated and Edited by Henry K. Beauchamp), (London, 1928), 3rd edition.
25. Edgar Thurston and K. Rangachari, *Castes and Tribes of Southern India,* (Madras, 1909).

26. Muthulaxmi Reddy, Sarojini Naidu etc.

27. Muthulaxmi Reddy's attempt to dispel the intensity or proportion of the custom in the region in her lectures in the west.

28. It is necessary to identify the emergence of the term devadasi, as deployed and popularized in the region. The paper does not deal with this specific issue however, I had discussed in detailed elsewhere.

29. B.R. Patil, "The Devadasis", *Indian Journal of Social Work*, vol. XXXV, No. 4, (1975); V. Ramakrishna, *Social Reform in Andhra (1848-1919)*, (New Delhi, 1983).

30. K.C. Tarachand, *Devadasi Custom: Rural Social Structure and Flesh Market*, (New Delhi, 1992), pp. 25-27. This work was specially examined as the theory of degeneration finds exposition and represents commonsense notions, values predominantly orienting collective consciousness in the region.

31. *Ibid.*

32. Priyadarshinin Vijaisri, *Recasting the Devadasi*, *op. cit.*, p. 41.

33. K.C. Tarachand, *Devadasi Custom: Rural Social Structure and Flesh Market* pp. 77-78, enumerates the list of major and minor deities that are part of the cosmology of the Renuka/Yellamma temple in Soundatti: Mallikarjuna, Parashuram, Ganapati, Akasha Barma, Uppina Basappa, Siddeshwara, Jamadagni, Harukellavva, Parvateshwara, Matangi, Bramhadevaru, Catri Deva, Markandesha, Kalinga Krishna, Sunkellavva, Kamashi, Minakshi, Durgadevi, Kedarlinga, Milarlinga, Marutidevaru, Channellamma, Jalari Devi, Dattatreya, Tulasi devi, Bhadrakali, Virabhadra, Annapurna devi, Mahasesa, Kamaratiyaru, Kutukadevi, Katadi devi, Taksaka, Huded Kariyamma, Ramalinga, Basaveshwara, Parasuramana Garu Ganapati, Matrutirtha devi, Kadalitirtha devi, Arishinatirtha devi, Siddeshwara guru, Jade Kariyamma, Naga Samuha, Kamadhenu, Kalpvruksha, Chintamani, Sidda Paduka, Airavata, Garuda-Sarpa, Gadha Brahma devaru, Sakshi Ganapati, Kalabhirava, Bankeswara, Mudalbhavi Kariyamma, Akasha Barma Devaru, Malleshwara, Talada Kariyamma, Saraswati devi, Ekinath and Joginath Maths, Jogulabhavi Satyavva, Ekinath and Joginath Padakatti.

34. For details see Priyadarshini Vijaisri, *Recasting the Devadasi: Patterns of Sacred Prostitution in Colonial South India*, (New Delhi, 2004).

35. Saskia Kersenboom-Story, *Nitya Sumangali: Devadasi Tradition in South India*, (Delhi, 1987).

36. Apffel Frederiqe Marglin, *Wives of the God-King: The Rituals of the Devadasis of Puri*, (Delhi, 1985).

37. The women said that traditionally they were expected to pursue their religious duties and when women volunteered to wok in their fields as wage labourers the employees refused to as they were apprehensive that it would invoke the 'kopa' /anger the goddess that was feared to be dreadful.

38. Jackie Assayag, "Modern Devadasis", *op. cit.*, p. 58.

39. *Ibid.*, pp. 58-59.

40. K.C. Tarachand, *Devadasi Custom: Rural Social Structure and Flesh Market*, *op. cit.*, pp. 14-15. Also see B. R. Patil *The Devadasis op. cit.*

41. *Ibid.*, p. 16.

42. *Ibid.*, pp. 382-3 and K.C. Tarachand *Devadasi Custom op. cit.*, pp. 96-97.

43. Meeting a group of ex-Jogati/Basavis on the 22nd of July was reassuring these facts. The group of women strongly held that Myrada introduced women to the term Devadasi and prefers that they use only identified as Sule, Jogati during the pre-reform period. Recorded interview at Mass Office, Ghattaprabha, dated 22nd July, 2004.

44. Mirea Eliade, p. 6.

45. Renuka is referred as princess of Kashmir, born to king Renuka on performance of a yagna. She is generally associated with Shakti goddesses.

46. Jamadagni was born to sage Kutika and Satyavati and related to Vishwamitra.

47. Svayamvara is a type of marriage in which the bride/often the princess had the right to choose her husband from among the assembled suitors.

48. Parusharam is considered the avatar of Vishnu in caste Hindu mythology.

49. According to other version she sees Kartavyavira in bathe in the river with his courtesans she is sexually excited.

50. P. Thomas explains the significance of the story of Jamadagni and Renuka as an invention to emphasize the absolute authority of the fathers and also as a clue to matricide in the ancient period, see his *Kama Kalpa*, *op. cit.*, p. 49.

51. Madhav Shastri Joshi (ed.), *Bharatiya Sanskrit Kosha*, (Pune, 1972), p. 86.

52. Mang is an outcaste leather working community, are believed to be the children of Matangi.

53. Wendy Doniger O'Flaherty perceives it as a tension between chastity and sexual impulse, which finally is resolved though ambivalently by the consequent split image of Renuka i.e., chaste mind and literally

polluted body, see p. 236. Significantly she links up the myth of "goddess who on transgression of chastity or lust are cursed to lowly or abnormal status" in the case of Renuka, this is evident in her bodily transformation wherein she is half 'untouchable' and half 'high' caste, see p. 218. Also see Dhere 1978: 61.

54 Jackie Assayag, "Modern Devadasis: Devotees of Goddess Yellamma in Karnataka", in Gabriella Elchinger Gerro-Luzzi (ed.), *Rites and Beliefs in Modern* India, (Delhi, 1990), pp. 53-65.

55. V. Lalitha, "Yellamma Worship – Village Deity (A Case Study of Jogins in Andhra Pradesh", *Proceedings of Andhra Pradesh History Congress*, (Warangal, 1990), p. 157.

56. Edgar Thurston and K. Rangachari, *Caste and Tribes in Southern India, op. cit.*, vol. IV, p. 317. A similar plot in Mala myth reported, Gotiayallamma, worshipped by Malas is the mother of the Pandavas and when Bhima threatened to kill her took refuge under a avireni pot in a Malas house. Eventually she was cursed to remain forever a Mala. *Ibid.*, p. 389.

57. Wendy O'Flaherty, *Sexual Metaphores and Animal Symbols in Indian Mythology*, (Delhi, 1981), p. 205.

58. *Ibid.*, pp. 205–206.

59. A. Madhaviah, "The Mathangi", *Madras Christian College Magazine*, vol. 23, (New Series vol. 5), (July 1905-June 1906).

60. David Kinsley, *Hindu Goddesses: Vision of the Devine Feminine in the Religious* Tradition, (New Delhi, 1987). p. 200; *Gazetteer of Bombay Presidency, Dharwar District*, (Bombay, 1956); Durgavva/Dyamavva – as incarnation of Parvati, p. 150; In one of the local myths, Durgavva, a Brahmin girl married to a Holeya (unknowingly) a Matangi's son. Eventually destroys her husband and children on knowing his identity. The killing reenacted ritually during the Dyamavva jatra, principal action being the Madigas who sprinkle the blood of the buffalo on sacrifice on the boundering to ward of evil. Madiga males perform naked rituals.

61. Wendy O' Flaherty, *Sexual Metaphores and Animal Symbols in Indian Mythology, op. cit.*, p. 206.

62. *Ibid.*, p. 211.

63. Emma Rauschenbauch-Clough, *While Sewing Sandals or Tales of Telugu Pariah Tribe*, (London, 1899), p. 54.

64. *Ibid.*, p. 57.

65 Mircea Eliade, *op.cit.*, pp. 6-7.

66. K.C. Tarachand, *Devadasi Custom: Rural Social Structure and Flesh Market, op. cit.*, p. 50.

67. N.D. Kamble, "Devadasis in Belgaum District: A Sociological Study", Un published Ph.D. Thesis, Shivaji University, (Kolhapur, 1988), the numerical strength of the women in Belgaum district was estin.ated to be about 5550 in 1985, pp. 11-12.

68. J.Assayag, "Modern Devadasis: Devotees of Goddess Yellamma in Karnataka", *op. cit.*, p. 55.

69. N.D. Kamble, "Devadasis in Belgaum District: A Sociological Study", *op. cit.*, p. 191.

70. K.C. Tarachand, *Devadasi Custom: Rural Social Structure and Flesh Market, op. cit.*, p. 85.

71. Marglin Frederique, *Kings and Wives:the seperaton of status and royal power, op. cit.*

72. N.D. Kamble, "Devadasis in Belgaum District: A Sociological Study", *op. cit.*, pp. 164-64.

73. K.C. Tarachand, *Devadasi Custom: Rural Social Structure and Flesh Market, op. cit.*, pp. 56-57.

74. *Ibid.*

75. Pauline Kolenda, *Caste, Cult and* Hierarchy, (Delhi, 1975), p. 147.

76. David Kingsley, *Hindu Goddess, op. cit.*, 216.

77. N K Kadetotad, *Religion and Society among the Harijans*, Karnataka University Dharwar, *op. cit.*, pp. 23-26.

78. *Ibid.*, pp. 206-207.

79. W. Elmore Dravidian Goda in Modern Hinduism, The Christian Literature Society, Madras, 1925. p 22-31 as mentioned in Saskia Kersenboom-Story, *Nityasumangali, op.cit.*, pp. 55-57. Also see Edgar Thurston, and K.Rangachari, *Castes and Tribes of Southern India, op. cit.* 1909, vol. IV, *op. cit.*, p. 296, Emma Rauschenbusch-Clough, *While Sewing Sandals, op cit.*, p. 70.

80. This job is also executed by a Mala headman, where there were no Madiga hamlets are available.

81. Henry Whitehead *Village gods of South India. op. cit.*, p. 73. For several such sacrificial rites through out the region see pp. 48-88.

82. *Ibid*, p. 52.

83. Suzanne Hanchett "The festivals interlude: some anthropological observations", in *Religious Festivals in South India and Sri Lanka* (ed.), Guy R. Welbon and Glenn E.Yocum, (Delhi, 1982), p. 220.

84. *Ibid.*

85. The virashaiva religious ideal of the mobile linga, perhaps legitimizes this fluidity in the custom in the region.

86. It was noted that women could demand a measure of grains during the harvest as their right. They maintained that usually it was left over food that was offered. On festive occasion when the women went around to beg they were asked to come the next day as they could simply not be given fresh cooked food.

87. N K Kadetotad mentions that 'Harijans go round begging at the time of community meals arranged in individual families and by veerashaiva monasteries during fairs and festivals. Usually, for (religious) begging they go only to the higher caste people; in, *Religion and society among the Harijans, op. cit.*, p. 23.

88. The Jogatis and Basavis begging in groups or in individually constitute a poignant memory of the outcastes in the region. Though it is not uncommon to find women on their begging rounds even today. For details See N.D. Kamble, "Devadasis in Belgaum District: A Sociological Study", *op. cit.*, and Priyadarshini Vijaisri, *Recasting the Devadasi, op. cit.*

89. Take for instance the state initiative in this direction, "Recently, a move that government jobs should be made available to non-harijans who marry Harijan girls. But this suggestion was neither popular nor caught the attention of the public" expresses how popular caste practices dabble with outcaste feminity and reinforces the idea of patterned access to female sexuality in caste cultures. As cited in N K Kadetotad, *Religion and society among the Harijans. Op. cit.* p. 29.

Index